Historic Towns of Hampshire & Surrey

Also by David W. Lloyd

The Making of English Towns
Historic Towns of East Anglia
Historic Towns of Kent & Sussex
The Buildings of Portsmouth and its Environs
Save The City: A Conservation Study of the City of London (General Editor)
(with Nikolaus Pevsner)　Hampshire (*Buildings of England*)
(with Donald Insall)　Railway Station Architecture

Historic Towns of Hampshire & Surrey

David W. Lloyd

Victor Gollancz Ltd
in association with
Peter Crawley

This edition first published 1992
in association with Peter Crawley
by Victor Gollancz Ltd,
14 Henrietta Street, London WC2E 8QJ
First paperback edition published 1993

Parts of this book appeared in *Historic Towns
of South-East England* published in a hardbound
edition 1987 by Victor Gollancz Ltd/Peter Crawley

A catalogue record for this book
is available from the British Library

ISBN 0-575-05276-7

Printed in Great Britain by
BAS Printers Limited,
Over Wallop, Hampshire

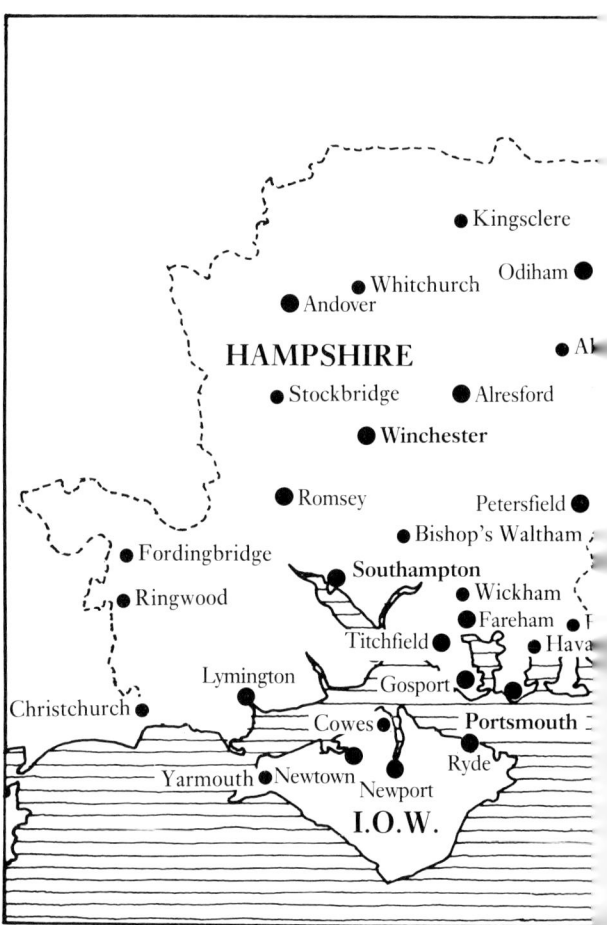

Previous page   **High Street,
Odiham, Hampshire**

Contents

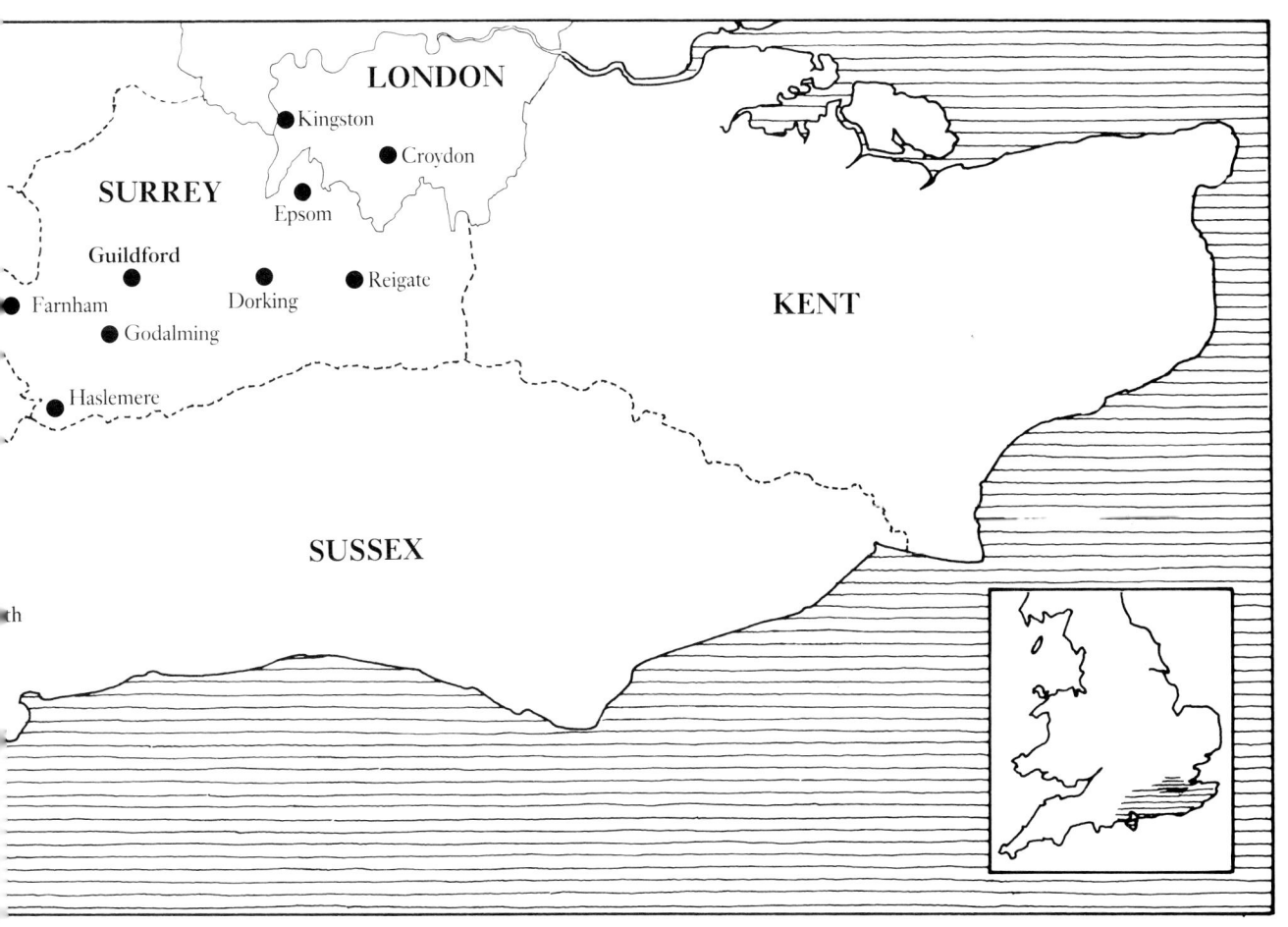

Preface

This is a revised edition of part of *Historic Towns of South-East England*, published in 1987. That book covered Hampshire, Surrey, Sussex and Kent. In 1991 a revision of part of it was published, in paperback, as *Historic Buildings of Kent and Sussex*. The present volume includes the remainder of the original book, with amendments, and the addition of a considerable amount of extra text covering twelve more places – Alton, Bishop's Waltham, Christchurch, Cowes, Fordingbridge, Havant, Kingsclere, Ringwood, Stockbridge, Whitchurch, Wickham and Yarmouth in the Isle of Wight – the Isle of Wight is taken, as it was historically, to be a part of Hampshire. Some of the earlier descriptions have been enlarged. I have respected the ancient county boundaries, including both Croydon and Kingston which, though now part of London, nevertheless retain a great deal of historic interest and individuality, as well as Christchurch which shamefully (I write as a Hampshire man) was transferred to Dorset in 1974. Inevitably the selection of towns for inclusion will seem anomalous to some people; there are certainly a few others which might have been included, but space is limited. I do not hesitate to include a few places now regarded as villages but which were considered towns in the past, and still look like old market towns, together with one place – Newtown in the Isle of Wight – which is the site of an almost vanished town which declined centuries ago; its town hall and grid of former streets, many now only tracks, beside its tidal inlet perpetuate the memory of its urban past.

The previous book followed *The Making of English Towns*, in which I traced the whole history of towns and cities, and was itself succeeded by *Historic Towns of East Anglia*.

All the photographs (except that opposite page 16, taken by myself) were taken by my publisher, Peter Crawley. The maps are from the early editions of the Ordnance Survey, dating from about 1870–90. Their original scale was 25 inches to the mile, except for that of Alresford which was at six inches to the mile, but they are not necessarily reproduced to the original scale. They are reproduced with the permission of the British Library. The photograph of Chamber Court, Winchester College, is published with the permission of the Warden and Scholars.

Introduction

Hampshire and Surrey may seem an odd combination, even though they have a common border of many miles. Historically they were united because they formed the ancient diocese of Winchester. Winchester is the prime ancient city in the two counties – a Roman town, the capital of the Saxon Kingdom of Wessex and the site of what was, until the Reformation, one of the richest bishop's sees in Europe. Southampton has the next longest history as an important place – as Hamwic it was one of the few significant trading centres in northern Europe in the dark years of the late seventh and eighth centuries. Later in the Middle Ages it was a major port with French and Mediterranean connections. The road from Southampton and Winchester to London was, by medieval standards, busy, and market towns developed at intervals along it – at Alresford, Alton, Farnham, Guildford and Kingston.

It is often asked, what distinguished a small town from a large village in the past? Except in ports, the possession of a market, usually held weekly but sometimes more often, was the most important factor which, before modern times, led people to call a fairly small place a town. At one time there were market towns every few miles except in thinly populated areas. Some of these, such as Guildford, had been important since Saxon times; others had markets which were set up under royal charters – which had to be obtained before markets could be started. They were granted to feudal overlords – who might be powerful barons, lesser local lords, bishops or heads of monasteries. The Bishops of Winchester controlled the markets at Farnham, Alresford, Fareham and Bishop's Waltham, all on their estates; the Archbishops of Canterbury that at Croydon, where they had a palace, and the Abbesses of Romsey the market outside their gate. In other towns, like Lymington, Newport on the Isle of Wight, Reigate and Petersfield, feudal magnates were in charge; in Wickham, a fairly typical example, the market and fair were started under a charter granted to the local lord, in 1268 (30). Fairs were annual events often lasting several days, whose main purpose was specialized trade, but which were also festive events; it is the latter characteristic which survives when ancient fairs are still held.

There were strong incentives for overlords to have markets and fairs, since they brought rents from the stalls as well as tolls on goods brought in and out, and they stimulated trade generally. As transport improved, many markets died out, and the places where they had been held often became, in effect, large villages, though still with the character of old market towns – Kingsclere, Odiham, Titchfield, Stockbridge and Wickham are examples (12), (26).

Some of the medieval markets began in entirely new towns, like New Alresford (Map I), and, very probably, Petersfield (Map V), founded by a bishop and earl respectively. The de Redvers family, Earls of Devon, whose local seat was Carisbrooke Castle, developed Newport (Map IV), Yarmouth and Lymington – the last two providing landing places, as now, for the shortest crossing to the Isle of Wight. They were also lords of Christchurch (a much older town) and patronized the priory there. At Farnham, a bishop laid out a wide street for a market, as an addition to an older settlement (4).

Markets were often held in wide streets, as at Andover, Stockbridge and Lymington (11); in widenings of otherwise narrower streets, as at Ringwood and Titchfield (**26**); in regular 'squares' as at Petersfield and Wickham, or in more irregular market places as at Kingston and Romsey (**17**). Stalls were normally removed after each market day, but in many places there came a time when they were left permanently, to be replaced eventually by substantial buildings. This resulted in irregular encroaching blocks, which are characteristic of many towns. Romsey originally had a large triangular market place, but it was partly encroached on centuries ago. The same happened at Croydon, where the medieval market place extended from High Street to Surrey Street – the present, daily, market is held in the latter, which is the remnant of the larger space otherwise encroached on. At Kingston the original market place, possibly of Saxon origin, was larger than now; the present space has permanent stalls – the survival, in modern form, of the earliest type of retail trading in the midst of what is now a huge metropolitan shopping centre (Map III). Epsom became a market town under a charter of 1685, and the open market is still held in the High Street.

Apart from Southampton there were many small ports on the Solent shores and creeks, which flourished at different times with coastal and occasional foreign trade, but they did not all grow into towns. Lymington and Newport were ports as well as market towns, while Newtown, on an inlet of the Isle of Wight coast, was ambitiously planned in 1255 as a port. The French sacked it in 1377, like neighbouring Yarmouth, and it never recovered; it is now a hamlet. Yarmouth recovered to some extent; it too has evidence of a medieval grid plan. Emsworth was a medieval town beside creeks branching from Chichester Harbour, but its heyday was in the eighteenth century and later with coastal, fishing, boat-building and milling trades – it has an altered tide mill which is one of the few surviving from many which once existed; another is at Yarmouth. Cowes grew into a town in the seventeenth century, and ever since has been engaged in the building and servicing of seagoing craft.

Portsmouth began as a small town founded at the mouth of its harbour in about 1180. The harbour was from early times a rallying point for ships on, or preparing for, warlike expeditions. The dockyard developed hugely in the eighteenth century, and was a major centre of skilled employment before there were any factories on a comparable scale. Very fine Georgian buildings, mostly of brick, survive, augmented by even grander Victorian ones, some of them pioneers in the use of iron. The Dockyard is away from the original town, and the Portsea district grew to house the employees in the eighteenth century. While Portsmouth expanded as a naval base, Southampton declined as a civilian port; by Tudor times its days as a European entrepot were over and its next role was as a Georgian resort.

The history of military defence is vividly illustrated in the area, beginning with the well-preserved Roman fort at Portchester behind Portsmouth, transformed into a castle with a Norman keep. Castle keeps also survive at Guildford (**8**) and Farnham, the latter the oldest part of what became a bishop's residence. Carisbrooke was the principal stronghold on the Isle of Wight. At Christchurch there remains a small keep and the shell of the very remarkable Constable's House of *c*.1160. Winchester retains the magnificent Great Hall of its otherwise vanished castle, while the bishops' fortified palace at Wolvesey near the cathedral is a substantial ruin (**34**). Winchester still has part of its city wall and its Westgate, but they are not as impressive as their counterparts in Southampton, which was vulnerable from the sea; the surviving parts of the town's defences are among the finest of their kind (**20**).

Henry VIII built a series of forts along the south coast; among them are Southsea Castle, Yarmouth Castle and the originally small Cowes Castle, now, greatly altered, the home of the Royal Yacht Squadron. Portsmouth was surrounded by low spreading ramparts on the Continental model, very different from medieval walls, in the seventeenth and eighteenth centuries; small parts survive (**15**), as well as similar though simpler works at Gosport. Finally, the 'scare' of a possible French invasion when Lord Palmerston was in power led to the building of the forts – magnificent in their construction, with thick layers of brickwork in conjunction with grassed earth, to resist explosive shells – on Portsdown Hill above Portsmouth and in Gosport (**6**).

Southampton still has the remains of many medieval houses, partly in stone and partly timber-framed (**18**) – including stone-vaulted basements, often where the houses have disappeared. (Guildford has two examples under later buildings.) The stone used in central and southern Hampshire until Tudor times came mainly from the quarries at Binstead near Ryde in the Isle of Wight, near which Quarr (i.e. 'Quarry') Abbey was founded – hence it is often called Quarr stone. The best stone from there is hard grey limestone, seen in Winchester Cathedral and Romsey Abbey, but there were also rougher, often brownish, deposits, used for instance on the Southampton town walls (**20**). A softer, greenish sandstone also came from the Isle of Wight. Caen stone from France was used in fine work, especially in the thirteenth century. Some rough sandstone was quarried in Surrey, notably Bargate stone around Godalming, while from Reigate came the soft, easily carved stone used in medieval London, as in Westminster Abbey.

But the nearly universal building material for houses right up to the early seventeenth century was timber. Until about 1500 most houses had open halls, with floor-hearths, from which smoke escaped through vents in the high roofs. From about that time chimneys (usually of brick) became general; they were inserted into halls which, then or later, were nearly always divided into two floors, while new houses were built with two storeys and chimneys from the start, often with jettied (overhung) upper storeys. At first, framed houses usually had their external timbers exposed, with plaster, wattle and daub between the timbers. By about 1600 it became common for structural timbering to be covered, either with plaster or, especially in Surrey in the eighteenth century, tiles (**9**). Very often timber-framed houses were thoroughly modernized in Georgian or later times; new façades might be added; older windows were replaced by sashes – so that a modernized house often gave no indication outside of its earlier origin. Many times recently the remains of older timber-framed structures have been 'discovered' behind later façades and partitions; Odiham and Bishop's Waltham have typical examples. Towns with significant timber-framed houses of up to seventeenth-century date, where the timber structure is evident from the street, include Andover (Chantry Street), Fareham, Odiham, Petersfield, Romsey, Titchfield, Wickham, Whitchurch (Newbury Street) and Godalming where, as at Haslemere, some of the old houses are partly of stone and partly of timber. Winchester has many old timber houses, variously altered, often with gables to the street frontage, and sometimes original bargeboards.

Brick was used in Farnham Castle in the fifteenth century, and for chimneys in the sixteenth – the ones built c.1540 when Titchfield Abbey was converted are splendid examples (25). In the seventeenth century brick became the normal building material. Whitgift's Hospital of 1596–8, amazingly surviving in the centre of Croydon, is built of it, as is the grander Abbot's Hospital in Guildford, started in 1619 (7). By the middle of the century there developed the 'Artisan' tradition, with bricks, often moulded and sometimes carved, forming elaborate patterns on façades and rooflines. There are minor examples in Godalming, Dorking, Titchfield and Wickham (31).

Hampshire and south-west Surrey excel in country-town houses of the broadly 'Georgian' type, though they may date from as early as the 1680s. At first they had mullioned and transomed windows (see illus. on back cover), but by 1700 sash windows became universal on medium-to-large houses. Bricks were made in nearly every locality, and until about 1800 they were usually of deep, bright red. But some bricks were baked so that the ends, at least, were greyish in colour – anything from light buff-grey to dark purple-grey, so that many 'Georgian' façades are partly of grey headers (bricks end-on to the façade), with red bricks round doors and windows and often on cornices; very occasionally façades are almost entirely grey (there are examples in Gosport and Havant). Chequer patterns, with grey headers alternating with red stretchers (bricks laid lengthways) are common. 'Georgian' houses generally tended to become plainer during the period; early ones often have carved brick details, and their windows are sometimes slightly arched, with or without keystones; later ones usually lack such features. Buff brick became a national fashion by c.1800, stucco soon after. Hooded or pedimented doorcases or, later, pillared porches are characteristic of the period. Of course, with the commercialization of many old streets, ground floors of houses have often given way to shops, while original upper storeys survive.

Farnham and Fareham are two towns with impressive series of Georgian houses; at Farnham in West Street and, more modestly, in Castle Street (5); at Fareham in the old High Street which, surprisingly in such a fast-growing town, remains remarkably unspoiled, with a memorable series of doorcases and porches. Other towns which have notable collections of 'Georgian' houses are Alresford (1), Alton, Cowes, Emsworth, Epsom, Kingsclere, Lymington, Newport, Odiham (12), Petersfield, Ringwood, Romsey (17) and Wickham (29). Winchester has a great many (39).

There are numerous former coaching inns with Georgian façades. (Sometimes they have courtyards which are partly older and always, if they are still hotels, they are extensively modernized inside.) Among those which contribute to the character of the streets they are in are the Swan, Alton; Angel and Danebury, Andover; Fountain, Cowes; White Horse, Dorking; King's Arms, Godalming; Angel, Guildford; Bear, Havant; Swan, Kingsclere; Angel, Lymington; Red Lion, Petersfield; Dolphin and White Horse, Romsey; Dolphin and Star, Southampton (19); Grosvenor, Stockbridge; Bugle, Titchfield (26), and White Hart, Whitchurch. A few fine bow-windowed shops survive, as in Winchester (Hampshire Chronicle), Ringwood, Petersfield, Fordingbridge and Dorking. Domestic bow windows are common in the south of England. Few date from before 1770; most are from the first half of the nineteenth century. They have local variations; some in Southampton are almost semicircular (**19**); in Portsmouth they are usually much shallower (**16**). The flat-fronted type, with canted sides, is common in Lymington. Newport, Cowes and Ryde have examples of each type.

Southampton was fashionable in the early nineteenth century, and has stuccoed 'Regency' terraces and villas (**24**). Even more impressive is the Crescent at Alverstoke, a suburb of Gosport, of *c.*1830 – the centrepiece of an intended resort. Ryde grew fast from about 1820, and has attractive houses, with one grand terrace (as well as a fine arcade), of the 'Regency' to early Victorian period. Portsmouth grew hugely in the nineteenth century; Southsea was at first a suburb, later a seaside resort. The local builder-architect-developer Thomas Ellis Owen laid out parts of Southsea, *c.*1840-60, as what we now call a garden suburb, with Gothic and Italianate villas disposed with deliberate informality amid greenery, interspersed with terraces. As Portsmouth expanded, the old town, hemmed in by its ramparts until they were removed in 1870-5, became more and more a backwater, while the present city centre developed outside the site of the ramparts. Despite devastation and rebuilding, it retains some fine Victorian buildings, notably the Theatre Royal. Meanwhile Southampton, re-established as a major port after the railway opened in 1840, also expanded (**23**).

Churches are major features in most towns. Medieval Winchester must have looked fabulous with its cathedral, two now vanished abbeys, its castle, its surviving college and peripheral St Cross hospital (**32, 33, 41**). At Romsey and Christchurch the cathedral-like monastic churches were saved at the Reformation as parish churches, but at Reigate the Priory is now the name of a fine later house on the site of the monastery. There are notable medieval parish churches at Alton, Fordingbridge, Godalming, Guildford, Havant, Kingston, Odiham, Petersfield, Reigate and Titchfield – the last is the oldest, with its Saxon western entrance, later heightened into a tower (see col. illus. opp. p. 32). St Peter's at Petersfield with its Norman details, and St Mary's, Guildford are particularly impressive inside. Portsmouth's parish church, part medieval and part seventeenth century, has been enlarged into a small cathedral. The best classical church – internally – is Holy Trinity, Gosport. There are fine Victorian churches at Andover, Dorking (with a beautiful spire), Newport, Ringwood and Ryde, and two splendid ones at Croydon.

Town and market halls make an interesting historical sequence. The Tudor timber-framed market hall from Titchfield was rescued from decay and is now, thoroughly restored, in the Weald and Downland Museum in Sussex. The Guildhall at Guildford is of earlier origin than its famous seventeenth-century front. Reigate and Whitchurch have small and attractive town halls in Georgian brick. At Newtown the Georgian town hall stands on the site of the vanished town – built in connection with the election of Members of Parliament for this 'rotten borough'. (Ten small towns, besides Newtown, probably deserved this designation, returning two Members through very few voters, until the Reform Act of 1832; Andover, Christchurch, Haslemere, Lymington, Newport, Petersfield, Reigate, Stockbridge,

Whitchurch and Yarmouth.) At Godalming the little 'Pepperpot' is the centrepiece of the town. Andover's classical Guildhall of 1825 dignifies the main street, while Newport has a handsome Guildhall by Nash, with a tower added later. Ryde Town Hall, as built in 1830–1, was surprisingly grand for what was then a very new town. Portsmouth built a monumental Guildhall from 1886, followed by Croydon in 1892–6 – Croydon is not all office blocks; they have wrapped round, rather than obliterated, the old centre, which has impressive Victorian buildings to a basically medieval street layout. Finally, Southampton built a grand Civic Centre in the 1930s when its prosperity, derived from liners, was riding the crest of the waves.

The Arts and Crafts tradition flourished in Surrey and the Hampshire borderland around the turn of the century. Painters like Helen Allingham, who lived near Haslemere, and W.H. Allen, associated with Farnham and Alton, painted cottages and farm buildings. Local architects studied vernacular buildings and designed in their styles, with varied success. Edwin Lutyens grew up in rural Surrey; his first creations were inspired by local traditions – like the house he designed on the outskirts of Godalming for Gertrude Jekyll, herself influenced by traditional cottage gardens. In Farnham the painter W.H. Allen was a tutor in the School of Art; one of his pupils was Harold Falkner, who became a prolific local architect. In collaboration with a local businessman, Charles Borelli, he restored many of Farnham's old buildings and designed new ones, often in impeccable Georgian styles. His masterpiece is the so-called Town Hall, dating from 1930–4, which not only accords with, but positively enhances, the townscape (see col. illus. opp. p. 16).

Farnham provided an example of how an old town of great distinction could preserve and improve its character in a time of change. Its example was followed a few decades later, after the introduction, or strengthening, of planning legislation intended to protect historic towns and buildings. The character of many places, has been successfully preserved: – village-towns like Wickham, Titchfield, Kingsclere, Odiham, Alresford and Yarmouth: flourishing market towns like Romsey, Petersfield, Godalming, Dorking, Lymington and Alton, maritime places such as Cowes and Emsworth. More substantial towns have managed to conserve their historic heartland, like High Street and Quarry Street in Guildford, the Market Place at Kingston and the old High Street at Fareham. At Southampton a surprising amount of the old walled town and its 'Regency' accretions survives; at Portsmouth the superb architectural heritage of the Dockyard is now becoming fully appreciated, just as its traditional use is in decline and its future in dispute. At Winchester, as elsewhere, there was some senseless demolition around the 1960s, but much of the historic city is now a model of urban conservation; some of the little streets south of the High Street and towards the College seem more attractive now than they were a few years ago.

For these achievements, credit must be given to some councils and their conservation advisers – notably Hampshire County Council and its Historic Buildings Bureau – and to the persistent efforts of local civic and conservation societies.

Alresford
Hampshire

Strictly New Alresford, this is a remarkable example of a planned medieval town. The Saxon village was Old Alresford, north of a small tributary of the River Itchen; the bishops of Winchester were its overlords. In 1200 Bishop de Lucy laid out the present town in the form of a T, the arms containing the main road from Winchester to London, the thick stem (Broad Street) the markets and fairs. Fires in 1689 and later destroyed the medieval fabric of the town but the street pattern survives. Most of the older houses are late seventeenth century or Georgian, but many of their brick façades have since been stuccoed or painted. Broad Street is delightful with its double line of trees; one of the best preserved earlier houses is on its west side near the bottom, with a façade of dark red and grey mottled brick, a wooden cornice and mullioned and transomed windows, characteristic of the end of the seventeenth century before sashes became universal (**2**). Beyond, the road narrows, twists and continues along an embankment, with a steep drop to the left and a lake on the right. This is really an earthen dam, built by de Lucy across the stream at about the same time as he founded

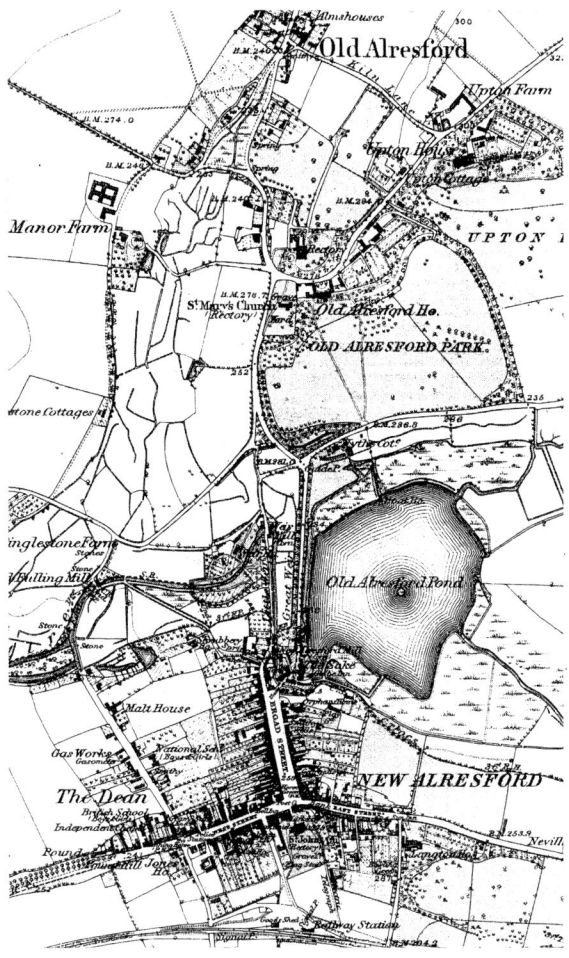

Map I **Alresford**. Bishop de Lucy founded New Alresford in 1200 south of the older village. He dammed a stream to form a large fish pond, and laid out the town to a T pattern, with Broad Street accommodating the market. The map is of 1870.

1 Broad Street, New Alresford. The town was devastated by fires in 1689 and later, and most of the buildings date from the last three hundred years.

the town. The lake so formed was almost certainly not intended as a headwater to help make the Itchen navigable, as is sometimes said, but to stock fish – an important item in a medieval bishop's household.

2 *Opposite* **House in Broad Street, New Alresford**, probably built after the fire of 1689; the mullioned and transomed windows are typical of the period just before the introduction of sashes, *c*.1700.

Alresford was a major wool market in the fourteenth century, and the name Fulling Mill suggests a weaving industry. The town was static from the end of the Georgian period until very recently; now its small shops do a good trade, making a pleasant contrast with the stores and supermarkets of the larger centres, and the branch railway, the 'Watercress Line', has been reopened by steam enthusiasts. (See colour illus. on back cover.)

Alton
Hampshire

Alton has a long main street, which was part of the medieval road from Winchester to London, and a coaching route in Georgian times. The street twists and dips slightly, with a great variety of building styles and shapes, at least over the shops. Early Georgian fronts in deep red brick, with strong eaves or cornices, are still prominent landmarks, but the most striking group of buildings is Victorian, in pungent Gothic round an open courtyard – all by Charles Barry, son of the architect of the Houses of Parliament. On one side is the Curtis Museum, displaying local history. It has an annexe, the Allen Gallery, in Church Street, with a collection of paintings by W.H. Allen, who for nearly fifty years from 1889 was tutor at Farnham School of Art. One of his pupils was Harold Falkner – the prolific and versatile architect who did so much to conserve and improve the town centre of Farnham (page 22). Allen painted landscapes and buildings, and was particularly good with vernacular houses, barns and farm buildings, inside and out, often with scenes of activity in vivid detail – providing invaluable records of the local countryside before it was transformed in modern times. His paintings – in oil – make interesting counterparts with the watercolours of Helen Allingham (page 30).

Beyond the Allen Gallery is the church, with what was the central tower of a Norman building, capped by a later spire, standing now to one side of an otherwise later rectangular structure – mainly of the fifteenth century. There are carvings on the Norman capitals under the tower with stylized birds and animals, and the pulpit is a particularly fine one which may date from the 1630s – but if it does it is surprising that it escaped

damage during the Civil War, when there was a skirmish in the church. The Quaker meeting house near the church, dated 1672 (though it has Georgian windows) provides a telling counterpart.

The Market Place is just north of the High Street, a small space which looked run-down a few years ago. Now it is attractively paved, and surrounded by restored, or suitable new, buildings. The Town Hall of 1813, islanded in the square, has been smartened, with shops in the arched ground floor which was originally open.

At the far eastern end of the town, past the turning to the station (the terminus of an electric line from London and, once again, of the steam-hauled 'Watercress Line' from Alresford, page 15), are two telling examples of social provision in the past. One is the former hospital of 1793 (close to its present successor), with a classical front thirteen windows wide – a surprisingly grand provision, at least externally, for a small town at the time. The other, just beyond, was till lately the grammar school founded in 1638 – the original building is of brick, with stone mullioned windows under gables; later extensions are in the same style.

The name Alton means village at the spring – a main source of the River Wey. There is still the King's Pond, south of High Street, but otherwise the town's watercourses have been modified or hidden after centuries of use for driving mills, tanning or making beer. Neatham, now an insignificant place to the east, was the site of a Roman settlement, and, surprisingly, of a market recorded in Domesday Book. It is not clear how and when Neatham declined and Alton became the market town for the area – as it certainly had by the thirteenth century.

Andover
Hampshire

The name Andover is Celtic, the second part meaning water, as in Dover. The town had a guild merchant in 1175, unusual for so small a place, and was one of Hampshire's ancient corporate boroughs. It had a serious

fire in 1434, and a few of the present buildings may date vestigially from the rebuilding. It was a major stage on the road from London to the south-west, and until recently the town centre looked much as it did at the end of the coaching era. In the 1960s the town was greatly expanded as part of the policy of dispersal from

London; large housing estates were built, industries grew, and the shopping centre was enlarged. Some effort was made to keep the main shape of the old town, and to preserve the dominance of the two focal buildings, the Guildhall and the church. The classical Guildhall (1825) stands effectively at the head of the wide High Street which keeps most of its old frontages; they bulge slightly inward on either side and broaden at both ends, to good effect. The narrow Upper High Street, largely rebuilt, leads to the climax of the church, successor to a medieval building which was unnecessarily demolished in 1840–1. It was designed by the little-known Augustus Livesay of Portsmouth (architect also of Newtown church, Isle of Wight), although Sydney Smirke supervised its completion, after trouble with the structure. The interior is magnificent, with lofty arches, high make-believe plaster vaulting, and chancel seen through an elaborate screen. Georgian and older buildings surround the church pleasantly; one houses the museum, with material from Danebury, an Iron Age hillfort a few miles away. The Angel Inn opposite the church has a Georgian front added to a timber-framed structure evident from the yard behind. Old inns are still a notable feature of Andover; the former Star and Garter in High Street, renamed the Danebury Hotel, has a splendid stuccoed front of about 1830 with very broad bow windows; the Globe has a Georgian front and refurbished yard. Other former inn yards have been adapted as footways off the High Street.

Recently, the Hampshire Buildings Preservation Trust has restored a range of jettied timber-framed houses in Chantry Street, which are now a landmark near the church.

Bishop's Waltham

Hampshire

Bishop's Waltham is a small town below the edge of the chalk hills, with sand and clayey country to south and west. It was the site of an early monastery whence St Willibald went in the eighth century, with other English monks, to convert the Germans to Christianity. Later it was held by the Bishops of Winchester, who built a major palace, ruined in the Civil War. More recently it was a centre for brickmaking and, for a period in the nineteenth century, the manufacture of terracotta.

The old town had a dense pattern of streets forming a rough grid. High Street is quite modest, leading up from the former market square (markets were held from the twelfth to the nineteenth centuries). Basingwell Street is to the west; Bank Street connects the two at their ends. All these streets have simple Georgian or Victorian, occasionally earlier, fronts – the local red and grey bricks are still prominent, although old brickwork has too often been painted over. Some of the façades – as so often elsewhere – conceal older structures; one house, on the corner of Basingwell and Bank Streets and another, with gables, at the west end of Bank Street, retain parts of medieval timber hall-houses, quite unsuspected from outside. Narrow St Peter's Street leads to the church, much of the fabric of which is post-Reformation – the tower of the 1580s, and the aisles of 1637 (north) and 1652 are all 'Gothic Survival'; the pulpit and altar rails are of the same general period. Little is medieval, but it is reasonable to suggest that the basic proportions of the nave, without its accretions, are those of a large Norman church.

The ruined palace stands on a site with long earlier occupation; the oldest visible parts date from the time of Bishop Henry of Blois (1129–71). The ruins are fairly dramatic, especially the tower like a small keep, and the great hall rebuilt by William of Wykeham, with its gaping windows – they should be seen not only from within, but also outside from the west, where they face a wood-fringed sheet of water which is part of the bishops' once larger fishpond.

The town has suffered from the requirements of the car. Probably unavoidably, the bypass severs the palace from the town. Less excusably, buildings were torn down in the most intricate part of the town, between Basingwell and High Streets, to create a car park under a dreadful plan of 1964. But Bishop's Waltham is still a pleasantly complicated place to walk about.

Christchurch

Dorset formerly *Hampshire*

Christchurch is, in a sense, one of the oldest towns in England. An important port developed in the late Iron Age on Hengistbury Head, on the south side of the small harbour – to which, among other imports, wine was brought during the early days of the Roman empire in amphorae, or ceramic jugs. Metals from other parts of Britain were exported. The Saxon town, a defended *burh*, lay between the converging rivers Avon and Stour to the north of the harbour; its long main street followed the same course as the High Street of today. A

Above **Farnham.** The town with its Georgian and earlier buildings was enhanced by the so-called Town Hall of 1930–4 with the arches and cupola, which fits in perfectly with the historic buildings. The architect was the local Harold Falkncr.

Left **Titchfield Abbey**

Overleaf **Castle Gate, Guildford,** the back entrance to the medieval castle (8). The old house, with tile-hanging, is now Guildford Museum.

church was built very early – the legend is that a mysterious workman helped to build it, disappearing at the end of each day; on one occasion a beam was found to be too short; it was miraculously lengthened one night and the workman – presumed to be Christ the carpenter – was never seen again. The present priory church dates from the 1090s – it was first built for a college of priests, not a monastery; the college was refounded as an Augustinian priory in 1150. It seems to have been well managed right up to the Reformation; the church was constantly added to and altered and is now one of the most remarkable in England, cathedrals included. The Norman nave has thirteenth century aisles; the Lady Chapel with its pendant vaulting was added around 1400 and the choir rebuilt in similar style just over a hundred years later. It preserves a superb fourteenth-century reredos with original carved representations of the Adoration of the Magi; the sculpture, vigorous and realistic, is among the best in England of the period. Nearby is the sumptuous chantry chapel, constructed during her lifetime by Margaret Pole, Countess of Salisbury, of Plantagenet descent and mother of Cardinal Pole who became the last Roman Catholic Archbishop of Canterbury under Queen Mary. Before then, he spoke vigorously against Henry VIII while a refugee on the Continent; Henry took revenge on his mother and had her executed in the Tower of London in 1541. She is said to have refused to kneel down to be beheaded, so that the deed was done while she stood. She was never buried in her prepared tomb; nor would it have been possible for priests to have prayed for her soul there, with the abolition of chantries. The choir retains its late medieval fittings largely intact – indeed this is probably the best preserved monastic church in Britain. One of its most intriguing possessions is a piece of wood high in a recess in the retro-choir, supposedly representing the miraculously lengthened beam of over a thousand years ago. No one has tried to establish the true age of the wood, nor how long it has been in its present curious position in a part of the church rebuilt after 1500. If it dates at least from before the Dissolution it is a rare survival of a sacred relic – this or a similar piece of timber was an object of veneration and pilgimage in the Middle Ages.

Christchurch had a castle, built by the de Redvers family, lords of the town as well as of Carisbrooke and Newport (page 34), and Earls of Devon. A small ruined keep survives on a motte, but the most interesting part of the former castle is the Constable's House, the fairly complete shell of a house of about 1160, of which the main room was on the first floor. Elaborate Norman windows survive, and a well-preserved round stone chimney is one of the oldest in Britain; two others of similar or slightly later date are in Southampton (page 57). The Constable's House stands beside a leat, or artificial stream, which was formed in the Middle Ages; it flowed past the priory, for which it acted as drain, and powered a still intact mill before entering the harbour. It runs for a short distance parallel to the Avon, which is crossed by a basically medieval bridge – the Avon and Christchurch have been famous for salmon since the Middle Ages. A path runs between the river and the leat, then curves round behind the site of the monastic buildings (which have virtually disappeared apart from the church), to emerge on the edge of the harbour where the River Stour flows into it – a wider river than the Avon, forming the boundary between Christchurch and its big upstart neighbour, Bournemouth. One looks across to Hengistbury Head and the site of the prehistoric port. Because the entrance to the harbour is very shallow, Christchurch never developed into a significant port in later times; the town became poor after the closure of the monastery, and did not grow significantly again until the late nineteenth century. Away from the priory and castle there are few buildings of note, but the town is pleasant, and holds its own against Bournemouth. The Red House museum, in what was an eighteenth-century workhouse, is worth a visit.

Cowes
Isle of Wight

Cowes seems to have taken its name from two former sandbanks which must have looked like recumbent animals when seen from afar. The name was used for two forts built in *c.* 1540 on either side of the entrance to the broad Medina estuary – which bisects the northern part of the Isle of Wight. One of these survives, repeatedly altered, as the Royal Yacht Squadron's clubhouse – the curved stone-faced platform overlooking the sea dates from then, but most of its romantic outline, with gables and turrets, is the result of a remodelling after the castle was taken over in 1855 by the Squadron – which originated a few decades earlier when yachting first became a fashionable pastime.

Cowes developed in the seventeenth century, with wharves and boatyards along both sides of the estuary. By the eighteenth it was a busy shipbuilding centre, and continued as such with the change to steam and steel. Its greatest period, industrially, was in the early-to mid-twentieth century. Local firms were innovators in the development of aircraft, especially those related to the sea; this tradition culminated with the Princess flying boat, sadly abortive commercially, in the early 1950s and continued with the building of hovercraft. Meanwhile shipbuilding, for the Navy, commerce and pleasure, flourished. Although one of the most industrialized places in the area, Cowes is hardly a typical industrial town.

The town is split by the river. East Cowes is unremarkable, until one reaches Queen Victoria's Osborne on its outskirts. West Cowes has the town centre which visitors see – mainly a long writhing High Street, with plenty of Georgian frontages in varied brick above small shops; those on the eastern side back towards the river. The buildings thin out near the Royal Squadron, where the shoreline curves to face the Solent. Easily missed – by those who want to explore the town – are Sun Hill and Market Hill climbing westwards off High Street, past picturesque, mainly Georgian houses, to converge near Northwood Park. This contains an early nineteenth-century mansion (now council offices) with a complicated history – there are surprising classical interiors. Adjoining is St Mary's church, mainly a nineteenth-century rebuilding of a seventeenth-century chapel, but including an extraordinary neo-Greek tower which was designed by the architect John Nash, partly as a mausoleum for the Ward family who lived in the house. (Nash's own country house, the romantically Gothic East Cowes Castle, was sadly demolished several years ago.) He also designed the fine classical former entrance to the park in nearby Church Road.

Croydon
Surrey

Croydon is a suburban city, with more offices than almost anywhere else except central London, and one of the biggest shopping centres in the south. But it has fine buildings, Victorian and ancient, which justify its inclusion in this book. The first syllable of the name is an anglicization of the Latin word *crocus*, which originally applied to the saffron plant, introduced to Britain by the Romans. It must have grown wild here when the Saxons arrived. From the Middle Ages till the eighteenth century the Archbishops of Canterbury had a palace at Croydon, convenient even then for London yet secluded. Parts survive, including the fifteenth-century great hall with its fine roof, and later parts in old dark brick. They were rescued exactly a century ago and restored as a school. Nearby St John's was the biggest medieval church in Surrey until burnt down in 1867. It was rebuilt impressively by Sir Gilbert Scott in the same Perpendicular style – unusually for him, the champion of earlier, 'purer' Gothic styles. The grand tower is medieval, with its tall pinnacles (heightened by Scott), and so is the porch.

A new traffic road swirls past the church, but pleasant small-scale streets lead to the town centre. The focus of Croydon must have moved to where it is now, on higher ground east of the palace and church, at least by the thirteenth century when the first known market grant is recorded. The market place was a triangle between what are now High and Surrey Streets – a steeply sloping site. By Tudor times the usual encroachments had taken place; up to a hundred years ago there was a dense and largely squalid concentration of buildings, threaded by alleys, in the old market area, leaving the present Surrey Street as the site for the stalls – where they are today, every weekday, selling fruit and vegetables. Nearly all the old buildings in the market area were cleared away in the 1890s and the site redeveloped, with a widened High Street – which, with its continuation North End, had already become a major shopping centre. The rebuilt part of High Street still has a lively and varied Victorian skyline above the shop façades, in contrast to the featureless redevelopment of the 1960s opposite. Down a side street is the ebullient Town Hall and Library of 1892–6, of red brick and stone in a Flemish style, with a tall tower that holds its own. In the very heart of Croydon is Whitgift's Hospital, an almshouse founded, together with a school, by an Elizabethan archbishop, with a dark brick courtyard of 1596–9, entered through a simple doorway from the street. The trustees have repeatedly resisted would-be redevelopers and street-wideners – but they have sold adjoining land, enabling the schools (there are now two) to flourish on different sites. Next to the hospital is the town's largest department store·which, with its early twentieth-century façade following the slight twists of the medieval street line, and its recent enlargement, symbolizes the steady, not sudden, evolution of Croydon from a small ancient town to a suburban city. Behind is the Whitgift Centre, on former school land. This, one of the earliest large shopping 'precincts', is still one of the most successful; it is neither brutal nor excessively brash, and it is well related to the older shopping facilities, of which it is an extension, not a replacement. Its most serious fault is that it ends with a mean back entrance in front of Croydon's most under-appreciated building, St Michael's church of 1883, a work of the great J.L. Pearson, architect of Truro Cathedral and many other churches – including All Saints, Hove, St John, Redhill (page 49), and St Augustine, Kilburn, London. Outside it is of brick with stone dressings; and the stump of a tower and spire which were never built is all too prominent. Inside it is superb – a lofty soaring space with a complexity of smaller spaces opening off. The church was always in a backwater, but it could have made the climax of the way through the Whitgift Centre. It is rumoured that a benefactor offered money to complete the spire to Pearson's design, but the church authorities refused, saying that there were other things to spend such money on; if so, they showed unforgivable philistinism. A soaring spire by Pearson would have held its own against, and set off, the office towers that now loom around.

The growth of Croydon as an office centre began in the late 1950s; since then a huge assortment of towers and slabs has risen to the east and south of the older town centre. With imagination as well as enterprise this could have become a miniature English version of parts of Chicago or Toronto, displaying something of the verve those places have. But it has not turned out so. Most of the office blocks are as banal as such buildings can be, impressive only because of their bulk. Almost the only one with compelling visual interest is near East Croydon station, with an odd polygonal shape, effectively seen at a distance along the Victorian street near the Whitgift Hospital. Twentieth-century Croydon is a huge opportunity missed; luckily much of Victorian Croydon, far more impressive, and even something of ancient Croydon survive.

Dorking
Surrey

Dorking is a market town with no spectacular history. It developed along the ancient west-east route under the North Downs, represented by the present A25, where it linked with a route from London into Sussex. It was prosperous in the seventeenth century, less notably so in the eighteenth, and grew only gently in the nineteenth. Today its growth as a commuter town is constrained more strongly than almost anywhere else because of the beautiful, varied and, on the whole, amazingly unspoiled country all round, the greenest part of the Green Belt. The town has a long, pleasantly writhing High Street which at its western, older end has a raised pavement on the south side, and still possesses more distinctive older buildings than nondescript new ones. Some are Victorian, with ebullient skylines; there is a fine double-bowed Georgian shop front in an otherwise late seventeenth-century façade. Elsewhere there are examples of mid-seventeenth-century brickwork with carved cornices and other rustic classical features, as in the narrow North Street, and in West Street –

which has a fascinating series of small-scale buildings, late medieval to Victorian, with old brick and tile-hanging still prominent. Alas, like the High Street it is plagued with traffic, since no solution has yet been found to the problem of the steadily increasing west-east traffic going through the town centre. The church, glimpsed occasionally down alleys or over rooftops, is a rebuilding of 1868–77 by Henry Woodyer, in dark flint with light stone dressings and a superb spire – the finest in any town covered by this book except St John, Redhill (page 49). The other Victorian surprise is Rose Hill, a housing scheme started before 1850, entered through a Gothic archway from South Street. There are varied, romantic, mostly gabled villas ranged irregularly round a rough, sloping tree-shaded pasture field, which is still grazed by horses; the best range is on the west side, where one of the villas is built of near-local white Reigate stone. The spire looms to the north. This delightful piece of early suburban planning – a smaller version of Decimus Burton's Calverley Park at Tunbridge Wells – ought to be kept intact.

Emsworth
Hampshire

Emsworth lies at the head of a long creek of Chichester Harbour. It was a medieval port, but most of its character derives from the Georgian period, when it flourished from coastal trade, boat building, fishing and flour milling. There were several mills, some on streams that flow into the harbour, powered in the normal way, but others were tidal – notably the brick, gabled Quay Mill of about 1770 which, recently converted, stands

conspicuously by the waterside. To provide power, an inlet was walled off by a curving causeway, now a promenade. The tidewater entered through a sluice, and the outward flow of the tide was directed to drive the wheel. There were tide mills like this at several places on the creeks and shores of the Solent coast, but few other examples survive (the best are at Yarmouth (page 77), Ashlett Mill at Fawley, and the small Eling Mill, recently restored to working order). Corn came from a wide hinterland, and some may have been brought by boat to be milled. By the beginning of the nineteenth century appreciable quantities of milled flour were sent by coastal vessels from Emsworth and other Hampshire 'mill towns' to London as well as to Portsmouth, where the Navy was a huge customer. Milling survived in Emsworth, at least for animal feeds, till quite recently.

Victorian Emsworth was famous for oysters, not only local 'natives' but also others which were trawled off the French and Portuguese coasts and laid down in the harbour at Emsworth. This needed boats of special design to carry the oysters back alive, and an Emsworth boatbuilder, J.D. Foster, produced vessels for this purpose which were, according to a local historian A.J.C. Reger, 'some of the finest working sailing craft which have ever cleared a British port'. Alas, the oyster trade suddenly ended in 1902 when a typhoid outbreak was traced to Emsworth oysters, and it never recovered. Today Emsworth again flourishes – but from pleasure boating.

The town has a spidery plan, with several streets and lanes leading to different parts of the watersides. South Street, the plainest, goes direct to the quay and former tide mill. Nearby Tower Street is a delight, with three or four of the town's best Georgian houses; it is a cul-de-sac except for a path which continues to the waterside. Queen Street also has good Georgian houses, in local red and grey brick. King Street has varied houses, including one which is (unusually for Hampshire) faced in boarding, with flat bow windows. This was built in 1795 by John King, a shipwright who did contract work for the Navy (it was him, not royalty, after whom the street is named). Emsworth developed after the parish system had been established, and had no church of its own till a small one was built in the eighteenth century, superseded in the nineteenth. For centuries it was in the parish of Warblington two miles away, where the church stands among fields, even today, close to a creek and adjoining a farm with a tall turret – all that remains of a Tudor mansion. The church is a delight, an amalgam of work from vestigial Saxon to high Gothic, and the churchyard contains some superb Georgian headstones with carved cherubs and classical decoration; one shows a ship sinking. There are similarly fine tombstones in other local churchyards, and one wonders if the craftsmen who carved them lived in Emsworth.

Epsom
Surrey

Epsom is a surprising place. It is linked to London by a sea of suburbia, yet it is a town of its own, with a working market place, and real country, including a half-wild common, pressing against its southern fringes. Epsom could argue with Tunbridge Wells that it was the earliest spa town after Bath. The remarkable properties of a spring on the common were noticed in 1619, when cattle refused to drink from it. Visitors came sporadically at first but in larger numbers after the Restoration – wealthy people from the City rather than aristocrats – but the arrangements by the well were rudimentary. Epsom was originally a small village, over a mile from the well, much less important than neighbouring Ewell. In 1685 a charter for a market was obtained and the present High Street developed; a New Tavern was built there in 1690 as assembly rooms. Soon after, a second well, supposedly with similar properties to those of the first, was opened on the edge of the town; the proprietor bought the original well in 1715 and closed it for a time, bringing the water from it in bottles to the new site. Epsom lost its reputation as a spa. But by then it was a favoured residential place. Already by the 1720s City men lived there in the summer and commuted by coach to London. Racing on Banstead Downs (as Epsom Downs were originally called) was an added attraction, especially after properly organized races were established in 1779 (The Oaks) and 1780 (The Derby). By the end of the Georgian period numerous comfortable residences were built in and around the town, and a surprising number survive (though there have been unfortunate losses recently due to demolitions or reconstructions, sometimes following fires). But Epsom grew completely informally. It has the straggling form of a rural market town, edging loosely to the west on to salients of its still partly rough common. The High Street should be visited on market day (Saturday) – Epsom is one of the few places in the south-east where movable stalls are still placed in their traditional locations. The dominant accent is the clock tower of 1854, richly vulgar. The New Tavern of 1690, later Waterloo House, was a very handsome building of which the upper floor survives, typically William and Mary with its ample pediment and decorative cornice, but a shop was first inserted in the ground storey in 1901. Now it is used as offices, and it is a pity that the ground floor elevation could not have been restored. Altogether the western part of High Street just manages to retain the character of a rough-and-tumble country-town street (despite a supermarket with all too typical sweeping roofs), while the eastern part, widened in 1938 and now mellowed, is in genteel neo-Georgian brick. The latest insertion is the Ashley Centre, a large shopping precinct set behind the buildings on the south side – rightly praised as good of its kind. Its visual impact on the High Street is positive – by one entrance is a strange octagonal tower with a conical top, just where such a landmark is valuable.

The Centre takes its name ultimately from Ashley House (in Ashley Road behind) of 1769, one of the best of Epsom's many mansions – Palladian, in buff brick (an early example of this) with a fine porch. Other fine houses are in Church Street, successor to the original village street. As the first part of this street has entirely lost its character, it is best to go from Ashley Road along an insignificant road called The Parade, passing two or three charming weatherboarded cottages – examples of several that appear all over Epsom: reminders of how rustic and informal the old town was. The Parade reaches Church Street at its most interesting stretch – there is a series of mansions, all set back in gardens, including The Cedars, with an appealingly awkward front, Regency Richmond House and the Old Vicarage, a William-and-Mary-type house from Epsom's heyday. The parish church (St Martin's) was rebuilt cheaply in 1824 except for the altered tower, but the inside is surprising. Sir Charles Nicholson –

later to enlarge Portsmouth Cathedral – extended the eastern part grandly from 1907 on, and the effect of the gimcrack Gothic nave of 1824 opening into the spacious and complex extension is impressive – although it was originally intended to rebuild the nave as well. Some charmingly sentimental wall monuments of about 1800 are by the sculptor Flaxman.

Other mansions are scattered around Woodcote – a loose-knit area to the south of the town. Two are on the Dorking Road (The Hylands and Hylands House), but the best group lies around the meeting of Chalk Lane and Woodcote Road, where there is a recognizable hamlet centre with weatherboarded cottages. Southward along Chalk Road one of the grandest houses, Woodcote Grove, is set back behind gates, while opposite, Maidstone House, a delightful smaller house, has Venetian windows on either side of its door. Chalk Lane continues past the large Victorian stables and riding school attached to Durdans, bought in 1874 by Lord Rosebery, racehorse breeder, Derby winner and, later, prime minister. The house looks relatively insignificant, but facing the road is a splendid iron screen, partly enveloped in vegetation, which originally came from Canons, the great house in Middlesex; it is probably the finest piece of craftsmanship in Epsom. Beyond is seemingly deep country.

Fareham
Hampshire

Fareham is a fast-growing town between Portsmouth and Southampton, closely related to both. But it is no upstart. There was a Roman settlement near the church, and by the thirteenth century the bishops of Winchester, as overlords, enlarged the original village into a borough and market town, with port trade on the tidal creek, an arm of Portsmouth Harbour. In Georgian times it was well-to-do, because of its trade and because senior naval officers and their dependents settled there, away from the raucousness of Portsmouth itself. There are two original main streets, High Street and West Street, forming an inverted L on the map. For well over a century commerce has been concentrated on West Street, leaving High Street almost unaltered in its Georgian form, apart from tarmac and traffic, and the fact that most of the houses are now offices or institutions. High Street begins beside an island block which separates it from narrow Union Street – representing an early encroachment on what had been part of the market place. Past the block the street opens out, and then climbs majestically to curve out of sight, with remarkable ranges of Georgian and earlier

buildings on either side. Four houses on the right form the show-group of the street. First there is Kintyre House, built in 1766 of grey and red brick with a magnificent pillared porch, the finest in an outstanding series of Georgian porches and doorcases along the street. Then there is No. 69, with a segmental porch, and a façade apparently of brownish brick which is in fact mathematical tiles, applied over the original red-brick façade in the early nineteenth century when red brick was out of fashion, even in Fareham. Next is a very fine house with two rounded bays, dated 1767, in the local Fareham Red brick, of a strong deep colour, which must have been made in appreciable quantities in the eighteenth century and on a much larger scale in the nineteenth, when it was used for important buildings in London (like the Albert Hall) as well as a great deal in Portsmouth. There is another good doorcase between the bays. The next house was built about 1830 in creamy buff brick, fashionable about then, with a striking elliptical archway and a little iron balcony above. The rest of the street has varied Georgian façades, some concealing timber-framed houses, and an unusually large number of small Georgian or Victorian paned shop fronts – illustrating how a country high street looked before many such streets became overwhelmingly commercial; houses of patrician size and interspersed with smaller properties where shopkeepers lived over their shops. The north end of the street – past an unfortunate gap that reveals the new civic centre – is of a generally smaller scale, and High Street proper ends beside the well-kept churchyard of the parish church with its work of many periods. As a final flourish, the Old Manor House lies a little beyond, with a splendid early Georgian brick front and another very fine porch.

West Street might almost be the main street of any town, but has one or two worthwhile buildings. The former Corn Exchange with a fine columned front, was originally designed in 1835 by the Portsmouth architects Jacob and T.E. Owen and extended in the same style later. Further on is Holy Trinity, the town's second church, built also in 1835 to the design of one of or both the Owens (page 47) with a marvellous interior – iron-framed, with slender piers and flat arches of 'Tudor' shape, a most elegant adaptation of the Gothic style in iron, with a slenderness which would be impossible with stone. Outside it is buff brick, with a stone spire. The nearby Westbury House has been opened as a very good local Museum. At the opposite end of the town, the railway crosses the creek by a fine viaduct of Fareham bricks – an excellent illustration of their deep red colour.

Farnham

Surrey

Farnham has a fine town centre which is largely Georgian in character, though its layout is medieval, and much of the town's appearance is the result of enlightened improvement over the last eighty years. There was a Saxon village, near which a Norman bishop of Winchester built a castle, overlooking the important route from Winchester to London. The bishops laid out the town as an episcopal borough, partly along the main road – a section of which is still called The Borough – and partly along Castle Street, leading at right-angles to their fortress. In the seventeenth century Farnham's markets prospered, drawing corn from a wide area. Much of the grain was carried on to Guildford, where some of it was milled and shipped down the Wey Navigation (page 27) to London. After about 1720 marketing patterns changed, and Farnham became more famous for hops; and it also had a coaching trade.

The view up the wide Castle Street, with its motley, mainly Georgian frontages framing the castle on its tree-encircled bluff, is one of the finest townscapes in southern England. The castle is unusual: there are remains of a polygonal shell keep (it has twenty-three sides) hidden behind the main range which faces the town. At first sight the castle suggests Georgian domesticity when seen from the street, because of the sash windows, but the tower to the left of the main range is a splendid early example of brick construction, now known to have been built by Bishop Waynflete in 1475. Bishops of Winchester lived in Farnham Castle right up to the 1920s – it lay in the centre of their original diocese which stretched from Hampshire through Surrey to the outskirts of London.

The frontages to Castle Street are not quite so consistently Georgian as they look at first sight. Some are refacings of earlier buildings, like the ironmongers on the west side with an iron balcony, while Lloyds Bank opposite dates from 1930–4. Further down, at the junction with The Borough, is a building with a tall cupola known as the Town Hall (though that was never its function), which dates from 1930–4. Round it is a group of buildings which provide the clues to understanding the present character of the town. Charles Borelli was a jeweller who owned and bought property, and cared deeply for the character of Farnham, which he sought to improve. In 1911 he restored 40 The Borough, which now shows an elaborate half-timbered front, with concave timber patterns as on the Welsh Border (of which there are other examples in the area, as at Godalming). It had been covered with a Georgian

3 *Left* Former Farnham Institute, South Street, Farnham, built in 1891, with lively representations relating to arts and crafts.

cladding of brick or tiles, which Borelli removed to re-expose and restore the timber-framing – a course which is against present-day conservation principles. Soon after, Borelli restored a smaller timber-framed building opposite, on the west corner of Castle Street, more conservatively, leaving the upper floor plastered, but setting the ground floor back to reveal the original jettying and expose the old curved brackets supporting it. These are among Farnham's few pre-Georgian buildings; from then on Borelli concentrated on conserving and improving the largely Georgian character of the town. In this his chief associate was Harold Falkner, a locally-based architect who, like his great contemporary Edwin Lutyens, brought up a few miles away, started by studying the old vernacular buildings of Surrey, and then came to appreciate more and more the Georgian heritage – this was the period when people generally were beginning to admire the long-despised Georgian style. Several Georgian buildings in the town were restored under Borelli's initiative or influence, usually with Falkner as architect – while Falkner also designed some new, convincingly neo-Georgian buildings (see colour illus. opp. p. 16).

Borelli's and Falkner's triumph is the Town Hall, which replaced a Victorian Gothic building which both considered unsuitable. Its style is that of about 1700, with sweeping but not over-prominent roofs, cupola and white-painted sash windows. The way in which it conforms with and yet accentuates the predominant character of Farnham, and provides the main landmark in the heart of the town, makes it a masterpiece when seen in its setting. On the Borough frontage the footway is set within the building, behind arches and a row of columns, and it is a fascinating experience to walk along it, under variedly treated ceilings with views across the street framed by the columns.

Some of the best Georgian houses are along West Street, the continuation of The Borough. Willmer House of 1718, now the museum, has an elaborate brick façade with rich decoration in its cornice, window surrounds and string courses; Nathanael Lloyd in his *History of the English House* called it 'perhaps the most remarkable elevation in cut and moulded brickwork extant'. Sandford House beyond dates from 1757, and the group is continued by Wickham House, whose façade was added in Georgian style to an earlier building by Harold Falkner – very typical. Little streets and paths lead to the church, a composite medieval building with a Victorianized exterior and a rather chilling interior where almost every bit of surface has been whitewashed – a practice now too widespread. The finest feature is the tower, which was left a stump at the end of the Middle Ages

4 *Top* **Farnham Castle,** built by bishops of Winchester, showing the 15th-century brick tower with decorative machicolation, and the wide Castle Street with a vestige of the market.

5 *Above* **Castle Street, Farnham,** looking down from near the castle. The street was laid out by a Norman bishop to accommodate the market, but the architecture is Georgian and successful Neo-Georgian.

but was heightened, very effectively, in 1865.

The best approach to the church is Lower Church Lane, a charming alley still paved with hard small pieces of ironstone – sandstone with an iron content, quarried locally; Georgian brick cottages frame the view of the tower. Southward from the churchyard, a path leads to the pastures which still border the River Wey, providing a foreground to views back to the town, much as at Godalming, and also helping to separate the town proper from its sprawling suburbs to the south.

(There is a similar partial definition of the old town on the other side by the castle and its park). Beyond the meadows and river, past a brewery and maltings converted into an arts centre, then across the roaring bypass, is William Cobbett's birthplace, a public house (it was not so in his time) which was for long, and very appropriately, called the Jolly Farmer; it seems inane that it has been renamed the William Cobbett.

The achievements of Charles Borelli as entrepreneur and Harold Falkner as architect make Farnham a remarkable early example of what in more recent times is called urban conservation.

Fordingbridge
Hampshire

Fordingbridge is a small, busy, straggling town beside the Salisbury Avon, close to the high, moor-like north-westerly extremity of the New Forest. It was called Forde at first, but a version of the present name was recorded in 1166, indicating that by then the original crossing had been replaced by a bridge. The present seven-arched bridge is basically medieval, widened and refaced; it is taken entirely by traffic and pedestrians cross by an abutting footway. The river seems very wide and natural to the south; the adjoining recreation ground has a bronze statue by Sir Ivor Roberts Jones of Augustus John the artist, who lived for thirty years near the town until his death in 1962. He is shown as if walking determinedly, looking intently at whatever would be in front.

The narrow main streets have many small shops – the place seems to thrive in a traditional country-town way – and too much traffic. Architectural interest is intermittent, but there is a notable series along the High Street going south, from a mullion-windowed seventeenth-century building to a grand Georgian house of seven bays, partly converted below to shops, and the turreted Victorian town hall. This is placed at the entrance to the small triangular former market place with its three public houses, one Georgian or earlier, the other two robustly Victorian. Provost Street, leading on, is uninteresting, except for a Georgian house with a well-preserved double-bowed shop front, until it crosses a stream – which flows east to join the river beyond a surviving eighteenth-century mill. Then comes the town's climax, on its far southern edge – the wide tree-planted Church Street ending at the parish church, a fine, under-restored medieval building of varied materials – flint, brown ironstone and Chilmark limestone. Mostly it is thirteenth-century, but the tower is Tudor and the north chapel has a remarkable composite roof, having hammer beams with carved angels which intersect curved braces with fretted tracery underneath – a smaller version of the roof at Bere Regis in Dorset. The nave roof is impressive but plainer, and the royal arms of George I over the north door is one of the best of its kind.

Godalming
Surrey

Godalming is set in the Surrey sandstone hills, where they are cut through by the winding valley of the River Wey, and by the steep-sided hollows of former tributary streams. The hillsides are still largely wooded even where dotted with houses, and the river is still bordered by fields. In the early Middle Ages it was an important village, the centre of a large manor and parish. It obtained a charter for a market in 1300 through its overlord, the Bishop of Salisbury, and grew mainly along the main route through the valley, later to become the Portsmouth road. Weaving developed by the sixteenth century, as in some neighbouring towns and villages; by the seventeenth Godalming was the chief textile town in Surrey; in the eighteenth stocking-knitting partly superseded weaving. Other industries developed, including paper-making and tanning; today Godalming has a surprising number of industries for a town of its type, some on or near old watermill sites.

The railway to Portsmouth gives a fascinating fleeting impression of Godalming as it crosses the Lammas Lands, described later, with a glimpse of the church. The station of 1859 is built of Bargate stone – a hard brown sandstone quarried in the vicinity, used in old local houses and much favoured by the Victorians. The church is not far away, also of Bargate stone, although the dates of the external parts vary from early Norman (the central tower) to Victorian (the nave aisles); the leaded spire is medieval with a slight twist in its timber framework. Church Street, leading south, is narrow and knowingly picturesque with buildings outwardly in stone, timber or brick, or hung with tiles, which used to give a rich and colourful effect, now much muted through too many of the surfaces being painted white. The climax is the 'Pepperpot', a delightful miniature former town hall of 1814 with a cupola, set in the confined space at the meeting of the streets which was

Map II **Goldalming**, when seen from the streets is a tight-knit town. But behind the long house-plots and yards, and beyond the river, is open pasture, giving the old town an immediate rural background just as in the Middle Ages. This map is of 1871, but the effect remains today.

the market place. The open arched space below is a good place from which to see the High Street. Behind the Pepperpot is a restored timber-framed building with a striking pattern of straight and curved members, reminiscent of the Welsh border country – other houses in this tradition are found in the nearby countryside, and also in Farnham (page 22). A more straightforward, but impressive, timber-framed three-storeyed house, the former White Hart inn, is on the south side of High Street. Further along the street, are interesting façades above shops. Two have weird seventeenth-century

patterned brickwork; another, handsomely Georgian with rusticated corners (above the shops) was an inn, while the King's Arms, re-fronted in 1753, is still a hotel. A few alleys and courts open into backland areas.

The old town is still compact, though long-drawn. The residential areas, many of them old-established, spread over the plateaux above the steep slopes on either side. On the outskirts to the south is Munstead, an area of former woody heathland, where the great gardener Gertrude Jekyll lived, latterly in Munstead Wood – the house which her friend and admirer the young Lutyens designed for her in 1896–7. It is built in Bargate stone with timber-framing, in the local vernacular manner which so influenced the early works of the great architect – who lived nearby in Thursley as a boy. Her garden has been modified, but the house is still set in thick trees, with the former gardener's house and a guest cottage, both by Lutyens, using tiles and timber, visible from the road. The nearby church is that of Busbridge, by Sir Gilbert Scott (1865) in Bargate stone with an elaborate version of a Surrey timber belfry rising from the centre. Inside is an intricate iron screen by Lutyens in the apex of the chancel arch; he also designed the strangely modernistic tombstone of Gertrude Jekyll and other members of her family in the churchyard. On the opposite hill, to the north, is Charterhouse, the seventeenth-century school which moved out of London in 1872. The older buildings form a remarkably impressive group in Gothic with a cluster of spires, making full use of the textural quality of Bargate stone, amply dressed in Bath stone for the detailed work. The chapel, with tall thin windows and soaring interior, was designed as a first world war memorial by Sir Giles Gilbert Scott, and is one of his finest works.

For a final impression of Godalming it is best to go to the foot of the hill on which Charterhouse stands, along Chalk Road, and look across the Lammas Lands. These were part of the original rural economy, parcelled out in summer for the hay harvest for people who had rights, and thrown open at Lammas, in early August, for autumn and winter pasture. They are still grazed, and provide a foreground to a view with the church spire on the right and the huddled roofs of the High Street area seen against the partly wooded background of the hill behind – a scene that can hardly have changed in essence since the Middle Ages.

In 1904 Gertrude Jekyll published a book *Old West Surrey* (since reprinted). It depicts, in affectionate detail, the cottages and farmhouses, their furniture, craftsmen's tools, and the way of life of their occupants, when the area was still overwhelmingly rural. One chapter is about Godalming. She refers to the 'Pepperpot', against the demolition of which there had recently been a successful campaign. 'The removal of this landmark of the early days of the nineteenth century would be a grievous injury to the town', she wrote, and continued: 'I venture to affirm that the possession of beautiful old houses, and of buildings not perhaps beautiful but of distinct architectural interest, is an important asset, even from the commercial point of view, of such a town as Godalming. . . . If Godalming is ill-advised enough to destroy the Town Hall or others of its interesting buildings, or to overload the street with architectural monstrosities so much out of scale that its good old houses are dwarfed and overpowered, the day will come when people . . . will say: "Oh, Godalming is spoilt; we will go somewhere else."'

Gosport

Hampshire

Gosport lies across the harbour from Portsmouth, a town of seventeenth-century origin with important naval and military establishments. Bombing and redevelopment have destroyed most of the old town; tall flats, roads and spaces have replaced old close-knit streets. Holding its own is Holy Trinity, originally built in 1695, enlarged in the eighteenth century and restored in the nineteenth, with a tall Italian-type campanile – exotic but very effective – added in 1889. The inside of the church is splendid with its Ionic colonnades; this must be the finest classical interior of any church in the area covered by this book. Behind the church are grass-grown earthen ramparts, parts of the defences of the town that were started in the seventeenth century but not completed at this end until about 1800; they are simpler versions of those at Portsmouth (page 41) and must be the last town defences (enveloping a town like medieval walls) to have been constructed in Britain.

Most of the circuit has been flattened; this stretch still looks impressive on its outer side, bending out into a bastion, with the recently tidied moat in front. Backing on to the ramparts by the church is the vicarage, built about 1800 of blue-grey brick, without the usual relief of red-brick dressings – to strange effect. Although intended at the start to be the vicarage it was taken over, when

6 *Right*   **Fort Brockhurst, Gosport**, one of the forts built round Portsmouth Habour *c.*1860 when a French invasion seemed possible. They are the last defensive works in the tradition of castles, with massive walls and vaults of brick, earthen ramparts and moats.

the ramparts were being built, as the residence of the local commander of the Royal Engineers – a post held for a time by Jane Austen's uncle; she is said to have stayed with him there.

Gosport is a town of scattered interesting buildings, only a few of which can be mentioned. The old railway station, opened in 1842, was built ambitiously because at first it served Portsmouth; now it is a complete ruin, but the long range of Tuscan columns in white Portland stone which formed the entrance remains, looking romantic amid the desolation. Various schemes have been prepared to incorporate this and other remains into new development, none so far achieved. Across an inlet is the Royal Naval Hospital, Haslar, built in 1746–61 when it was the largest hospital in Europe and the biggest brick building in England. The architect was Theodore Jacobsen, who had previously designed the now vanished Foundling Hospital in Bloomsbury, London. Up to two thousand patients were accommodated here in the early years of the hospital, and the physician in charge from 1758 was Dr Lind, one of the outstanding medical men of the time, who had a great influence on conditions in the Royal Navy. There have been big recent additions, but the magnificent façade, with sculptured figures representing navigation, and the royal coat of arms, is unaltered.

Alverstoke was the original village and parish before Gosport grew. A local entrepreneur tried to promote it as a resort with, as its centrepiece, a splendid Crescent of about 1830, a stuccoed composition as fine as anything of its kind in Brighton, with Doric columns, made of iron but painted, along the ground storey. It is to be found amid quiet suburban roads (Crescent and St Mark's Roads), near Alverstoke church, a Victorian rebuilding by Henry Woodyer (architect also of Dorking church), with a highly individualistic interior – the tower is later, not by him. Finally, towards Fareham is Fort Brockhurst, one of several Victorian forts built across the Gosport peninsula in the 1850s to protect Portsmouth against possible invasion by the French – similar to the slightly later ones along Portsdown Hill (page 43) but, being low-lying, having wet moats, not dry ones. It used to look picturesque with vegetation growing round the moat and elsewhere; now it is an ancient monument, restored to mint condition, displaying some of the most massive brick construction ever achieved. A bomb partly destroyed a vaulted chamber and revealed eight courses of brickwork supporting several feet of earth, on which were mounted heavy guns.

Guildford

Surrey

Guildford is entangled by traffic routes and dominated by crude commercial development. Or so it might seem to people approaching from many directions, especially from the station. But behind the swathe of crude mid-twentieth-century rebuilding there is still a historic town of rare and concentrated interest. It is best to get, by whatever means, into the High Street, with its dramatic views up and down. It was part of an ancient route which crossed the River Wey where it flows through a steep-sided gap in the chalk hills. Guildford was already a town in the tenth century when it had a mint; the High Street with its long, narrow-fronted house plots may have been laid out then or, at the latest, in the Norman period when the castle was built. By Tudor times the town flourished through weaving; in the seventeenth century, especially after the opening of navigation along the canalized River Wey in 1653, it became a distribution centre for the area. In Georgian times, the growth of Portsmouth dockyard made it an

important transit town on the way there. Like many ancient streets where each plot has its own building history, the High Street has a great variety of architecture over several centuries. There are two medieval stone undercrofts, unseen from the street, one in the Angel

7 *Right* **Abbot's Hospital, Guildford,** founded in 1619 by a local man who became archbishop.

Hotel; several gabled overhung timber-framed houses, their upper storeys plastered over (the ground storeys are all shops); many Georgian façades and ebullient Victorian compositions; the worst recent intrusions are at either extremity. But the three most striking buildings in the street are from the town's architectural heyday, the seventeenth century. First there is Abbot's Hospital, an almshouse founded in 1619 by Archbishop George Abbot, of humble Guildford origin. It has a great brick entrance tower with corner turrets, a late example of the Tudor gatehouse tradition, leading to a courtyard like that of an Oxford or Cambridge college. Second, and very different, is Guildford House (as it is now called), further down High Street, built, or remodelled,

8 *Left*   **Guildford Castle.** The keep was built *c.*1170 on an older earthen motte; some of the windows were altered in Tudor times.

9 *Below*   **Quarry Street, Guildford.** In the foreground the 13th century Castle Arch. Adjoining is Guildford Museum, in a picturesque 17th century and later building of local brick, sandstone and tiles.

10 *Opposite*   **High Street, Guildford,** still a marvellous street in its well-protected central part, with varied frontages of the 17th to 20th centuries over the ground-floor shops. The climax is the cupola and clock of the Guildhall at the brow of the hill.

in 1660. It is extremely interesting as a small but elaborate town house of the period, possibly like many built in London just before the Great Fire. It is in a mercantile Renaissance style, with large transomed windows of small leaded panes and later, Georgian, shop windows; inside are a fine staircase and ceilings. Finally there is the Guildhall, an older building to which the façade was added in 1683, with mullioned leaded windows on the upper floor (bigger than those on Guildford House), an iron balcony for proclamations,

and a cupola. 'The effect is more like the poop of a seventeenth-century ship than anything else' wrote Ian Nairn in *The Buildings of England: Surrey*. What makes the Guildhall specially memorable is the clock, projecting from a beam over the pavement, *the* landmark of the street, since it is on the brow. The view down is memorable also for the green slope of downland, crested by a strip of woodland, which is still the closing feature, meticulously conserved by councillors and their planning advisers through ensuring that undesirable buildings were kept just out of sight to left or right.

Narrow streets and alleys lead off the High Street; the best by far is Quarry Street, passing St Mary's, the only one of three churches of ancient foundation not rebuilt since the Middle Ages. It has a beautiful interior, predominantly transitional from Norman to Gothic, with a vaulted eastern part; built internally of chalky stone which may have come from the old quarry to which the street led. The small flinty tower is late Saxon. Quarry Street leads on past varied houses to the Castle Arch, adjoining a house in the Surrey vernacular style which is now the local museum (see colour illus. opp. p. 17). Through the arch is the still impressive castle keep, built about 1170 on earlier earthworks, mainly of dark sandstone from the hills to the south. On the other side of Quarry Street, a steep path called Rosemary Alley descends between houses, revealing their colourful brick and tiled backs, to a busy road, across which is the Yvonne Arnaud Theatre. The theatre was one of the fruits of Guildford's prodigious period in the 1960s, which saw the completion of the cathedral and the foundation of the university, as well as the erection of many ugly buildings. It is a pleasant informal modern building set among trees by the River Wey, grouping with an almost monumental former mill in Georgian and Victorian brick.

It is possible to walk from here, near the river, through a semblance of country which fairly soon broadens into real country – Guildford has been restrained from growing too far to the south. Across the river is a still attractive, very informal area with old villagy houses and Victorian villas, some in sandstone or tile-hung, overshadowed by two appallingly inept lumps of multi-storey offices – they may be out of sight from the High Street, but nearer at hand they disjoint their surroundings. Buildings like this, bad in themselves and disastrously placed, stand in perpetual condemnation of the developers who promoted them, the architects who designed them, the councillors who permitted them, and possibly the planners who advised the councillors (unless the last advised otherwise and were overruled, as sometimes happens). Luckily these are not the only prominent buildings of the twentieth century in Guildford. It was a very brave decision to build a cathedral when a new diocese was formed between the wars, rather than tinker with an unsuitable parish church, as happened at Portsmouth. A hilltop site was chosen on the edge of the town – sadly difficult to reach from the centre of the town but topographically superb. The architect, Sir Edward Maufe, produced one of the last triumphs of the Gothic Revival, started in 1936, finished thirty years later. If Gothic is primarily a style of external massing and internal enclosure of space, then Guildford is a splendid example. Outside it is stark and soaring, in local pale red brick, culminating in a tower which is just right in relation to the rest. Inside there is a majestic main space, with narrow aisles and other side spaces to provide a variety of vistas. But the details and fittings are sparse and, on the whole, not of great merit. The University of Surrey was formed from an older college which moved out of London in 1968 to a site on the slope north-east of the cathedral. The buildings, by the Building Design Partnership, are in one of the more acceptable manners of the sixties, amenable rather than aggressive, placed with contrived irregularity on the slope with patches of lush landscape in between, and gaps for occasional glimpses of the cathedral. Pale brick predominates; no harsh concrete. So Guildford gained more in the sixties and seventies than traffic gyratory systems, shopping 'precincts' that might be anywhere, and intrusive office blocks. The preservation of at least part of the High Street is a major triumph. So is the fact that it is still not too difficult to walk from the town into fine country in some directions.

Haslemere
Surrey

Haslemere was a remote town in the hills, which probably first developed in the thirteenth century when the bishop of Salisbury, lord of the huge manor of Godalming of which it was on the edge, gained a grant for a market. In 1596, for no very clear reason, Queen Elizabeth gave it the right to send two members to Parliament. Voters were the freeholders of the burgage plots, and this gave rise to a great deal of abuse. From the 1780s, the Lowther family, Cumberland landowners, tried to control the voting by buying burgage plots and granting temporary freeholds to miners and other employees, whom they brought south and installed as residents at the right times for the elections. (Probably Haslemere was the first place where coal miners were able to vote.) Between 1832, when rotten boroughs were abolished, and 1859, when the railway to Portsmouth was opened, Haslemere relapsed into obscurity. After that, literary and artistic people, as well as simple life idealists, were attracted to the locality. Tennyson settled at Aldworth in the hills to the south. A group of artists formed what eventually became the Haslemere Society of Artists; the best known was Birket Foster, who actually lived in nearby Witley. Helen Allingham came to Witley with her husband in 1875 and became associated with the society; she, like the others, were attracted by the landscape and vernacular buildings. She painted local cottages with their weathered textures of timber, brick and stone, patchy colourwashing, tile-hanging, and irregular roofs in tiles or Horsham slabs, always with authentic cottage gardens and posed figures in rustic dress. Her paintings are enchanting, and show idealistically but not unrealistically what the south Surrey countryside was like before the stockbrokers arrived. It was the same world which captivated the young Edwin Lutyens and Gertrude Jekyll.

Haslemere also became a place for crafts. Enthusiasts set up workshops for weaving and other activities, and these flourished up to the first world war. At the end of the war, Arnold Dolmetsch settled in the town; he opened workshops for making musical instruments and instituted the local music festival. Another local institution is the Educational museum. This originated with Sir James Hutchinson, a surgeon who was a Quaker and a friend of Tennyson; he came to the area in the 1860s, formed a private museum and encouraged local interest in the history of mankind. His collection moved to its present location in a converted house in 1926. In its final form it attempts to portray the evolution of the world and the history of humanity. From Hutchinson's time it set out to encourage parties of children to come and learn, and in this it was a pioneer. It still seems remarkable for the breadth of its vision.

Haslemere has few notable buildings but much charm. The old town centre is, on the whole, unsullied, with a widening main street descending to a simple market hall of 1814 – scene of the last corrupt elections – and narrower streets leading off. There are still vernacular buildings with something of an Allingham quality, though without cottage gardens, and there are self-consciously picturesque rebuildings from the arts-and-crafts era, as well as two or three urbane Georgian fronts. Appropriately the Museum building with its pillared porch is the chief accent in the northern part of the High Street where it narrows and climbs. Haslemere has grown significantly in only one direction – westwards past the station. In other directions there is glorious country – the sandy Surrey hills, the bolder Sussex hills towards Midhurst, the Weald to the east.

Havant
Hampshire

Havant is a much more interesting town than one might expect, given the growth of the area, adjoining Portsmouth, since 1945: the town proper is still a market town in feeling, with a straightforward cross pattern of streets. The best is East Street, slightly sinuous with some good Georgian buildings, notably the Bear hotel, almost entirely in grey bricks except for the tops of the window openings which are in red, and Magnolia House (no. 27), in pale grey bricks with much more profuse red brick dressings, and a pillared porch. Behind an adjoining house, itself Victorian, is a Georgian brick gazebo, or summer house, seen from the street behind – which is curiously called The Pallant, reminiscent of nearby Chichester. Further west along The Pallant (nearly at its junction with North Street) is a one-time Congregational chapel, now used commercially, with a fascinating front of 1718, in chequer brick with a device like a blank 'Venetian' window on the roofline, its details carved in brickwork – a nice rustic jumble of classical motifs.

The central crossroads is defined by two striking Victorian buildings – the gabled White Hart of 1889 on one corner and a solid Italianate block opposite, with its original round-arched shop front. A third corner is taken by the churchyard, with the church admirably placed – a mixed building of which the western part is a Victorian reconstruction and the eastern part is medieval – with a very fine thirteenth-century vault over the chancel. The crossing arches have interesting Norman-style carvings which are partly original. South-east of the churchyard is another fascinating corner – Homewell. Here is a pond fed by a spring which gave Havant its name, Hama's 'fount', first recorded in 935. The water has qualities which made it suitable for the manufacture of parchment from sheepskins – a local industry for many centuries. The last parchment firm, Stallards, which closed in 1936, occupied the brick buildings behind the pond, not architecturally notable but of great interest in industrial history.

Havant was probably the site of a small Roman town, and then a Saxon village. It grew into a town again after a market was established in 1200, and had its own little port just over a mile away at Langstone, bordering the creek which separates Hayling Island from the mainland. (Langstone gave its name to the large harbour to the west, through which some vessels would have approached it.) Today Langstone, severed from the town proper by the bypass, has a picturesque open quay, with two public houses and, at the end, an extraordinary former mill, now a house. The main part was a water mill, but attached was a windmill, the hollow-sided cone of which survives, without its sails, looking like a lighthouse. From the mill there is a short shoreside walk to the lonely church of Warblington, described in the account of Emsworth (page 20).

Kingsclere

Hampshire

Kingsclere is a former market town, now a large village. It is very much centred on its church, which looks gauntly Norman. In fact much of its appearance dates from a restoration of 1848–9, when the architect Thomas Hellyer of Ryde removed many later accretions and substituted neo-Norman work, including the top of the tower – which, however, stands on internal arches which are basically genuine even if mostly renewed. Swan Street leading south is a delightful street where many of the older, Georgian, buildings are in a combination of deep, purply-grey brick with bright red brick for window surrounds and dressings; others have chequer patterns in the two colours. The highlights architecturally are the early-eighteenth-century Swan hotel, and a grand house across the street further down, the latter lately extended and split into offices. The street thins out into the undulating clayey countryside, with the clear grass escarpment of the chalk downs rising a mile or two to the south. A different, quieter thoroughfare is North Street, ending with a small group of buildings in the same combination of bricks, including a Victorian school.

Kingston

Surrey

Kingston upon Thames is memorable for its market place. There was a market in the thirteenth century, but the town was important long before that. The claim that six Saxon kings were crowned there between 902 and 958 is authentic – but why? Possibly because it was a river crossing linking the ancient kingdom of Wessex with what had been Mercia. When a bridge replaced the ford over the Thames is not known – certainly by 1193: for centuries it was the first one up-river from London Bridge. From being a small but busy market town, Kingston has grown into a huge suburban shopping centre. Yet amazingly the market is still the essence of the place. It is an irregular triangle, with an islanded former town hall, Italianate of 1838, for some reason painted blue-grey (it is really of stock brick). The Georgian tower of the church (which has a fine medieval interior) rises behind the buildings on the north side. The buildings are a market-town miscellany – the best are Edwardian on the north-west corner. One built by Boots (they are no longer there) is a splendid neo-Tudor confection with statues illustrating Kingston's history; the other, to the left, over a modern shop and now brightly painted, was a fashionable restaurant built in 1901. In between, on the corner, is a building genuinely of *c.*1590 with wooden classical pilasters. Beyond the southern apex of the market place rises the brick and stone Guildhall of 1935 by Maurice Webb, solid and circular; its massive tower complements that of the church at the other end of the market. In front is what is supposed to be the Saxon coronation stone, protected by Victorian railings. Nearby flows the small Hogsmill river, a tributary of the Thames, crossed by Clattern Bridge – inconspicuous from the Guildhall side. But if one goes to the other side of the bridge,

Map III **Medieval Kingston** is very apparent on this map of 1868, and much of the layout survives today round the Market Place – which must originally have included the smaller Apple Market to the east, until encroaching blocks of buildings separated the latter from the main market area. Clattern Bridge, over a tributary of the Thames to the south-west, still has medieval arches under the modern roadway.

and down steps to a streamside path, one sees that the two arches are of medieval stone, apparently little restored, and are said to date from the late twelfth century – if so, is this the oldest bridge in Britain? (The bridge was originally much narrower and has been widened towards the Guildhall.) Related to the market

Previous page **Church Street, Titchfield.** The lower part of the church tower was originally a Saxon porch, heightened in the 13th century with the spire added later.

Left **High Street, Winchester.** Buildings date from the Middle Ages onwards, often older behind their Georgian or later façades. In the distance the restored 15th-century Butter Cross, and in the background the green hill which closes the view down the street.

Below **The Deanery, Winchester.** A very complicated building, adapted from the 13th-century Prior's Lodging, with a brick wing in the background added in the reign of Charles II.

place on its eastern side, and connected by an alley, is the tiny Apple Market, really the widening of a lane. Undoubtedly the market place originally extended to the Apple Market and its associated lane, and the buildings in between represent early encroachments.

The market place with its medieval form and feel is contrasted by the busy shopping centre to the north – Thames Street provides the transition. Bentall's huge department store of the 1930s has been redeveloped, but keeping the great, partly curved frontage of brick and stone by the same architect as the Guildhall, reminiscent of Hampton Court. In further contrast is the new John Lewis store by the river, a complex, romantic-modern building with a jostling skyline, where orange-buff brick counterparts stretches of glazing. Unfortunately the brickwork is too uniform and forbidding on the Clarence Street frontage. The store adjoins Kingston Bridge, late Georgian but widened (the medieval bridge was a little further downstream). The former river frontage on either side was simply commercial backland; redevelopment to the south has opened up the waterside, with a green view across the river to the beginning of Hampton Court park.

Lymington

Hampshire

Lymington is traditionally the market town for the New Forest, but in origin it was a port, as it still is today – for the crossing to the Isle of Wight. But the present pier for the Island ships is on the other side of the harbour from the town, and thousands pass Lymington without seeing more of it than a view across the harbour – which is the tidal estuary of a small river flowing from the Forest. As a town it dates from around 1190–1200 when William de Redvers founded a new borough. The Redvers were earls of Devon and lords of the Isle of Wight; they were also overlords of Christchurch. They founded new boroughs on either side of the shortest crossing to the Island – at Yarmouth as well as Lymington – and William's predecessor, Richard de Redvers, founded Newport near his castle at Carisbrooke (page 34). Medieval Lymington developed wider trade; it imported wine and exported cloth from Salisbury, but in this respect it was insignificant compared with Southampton. But the area was very important for salt production from the Middle Ages until the early nineteenth century; sea water was impounded near the coast, allowed to evaporate partially in the sun, and then, as brine, boiled in metal-lined containers fuelled with wood or, later, coal brought coastwise. Shipbuilding was an old-established industry, and specifically yacht-building began in the early nineteenth century; now Lymington is a major centre for pleasure boating. It was already a favourite place of residence for the retired, or those of private means, in the eighteenth century, which partly explains the number of fine Georgian houses.

Apart from the harbourside, old Lymington is nearly all one long street. From the open quay a narrow street leads to the lowest part of the main street, Quay Hill, self-consciously pretty with cobbles, and some fine bow windows. The High Street was almost certainly laid out at the foundation of the town. It is a classic example of a medieval market street – broad to accommodate the stalls, and with a pattern of deep house plots, still very evident (though they vary in width) on either side. It climbs steadily at first, then levels off. The gradient has been lowered towards the top of the slope, leaving pavements on either side following the original levels, to very good effect. Until 1855 a market hall stood in the street just at the brow; now the wide street continues uninterrupted to the church, which comes into view as one reaches the flatter stretch. Lymington should be seen on Saturday – market day. The stalls are still disposed along the street as they have been since the thirteenth century, though they are now only one deep – possibly there were more rows in the past. Architecturally the street is a pleasant medley in style and scale. Nothing obvious survives from before the late seventeenth century, though there may be older structures behind façades. As in most

11   **High Street, Lymington** on market day – the wide street was laid out about 1200 to accommodate markets like this.

streets of medieval origin, every plot has its own particular building history, and in Lymington it is specially rewarding to follow the sequences on either side of the street. Many of the buildings are two-storeyed and modest, but some of the Georgian ones are grander, of three storeys or even more. They nearly all have shops in the ground floors – some are fairly intrusive, but a few are attractive, notably No. 41/2 with its Victorian ironwork. The Angel hotel has a first-floor iron balcony, and so has a bank. Many upper storeys have Georgian bow windows; in Lymington flat-fronted ones with canted sides are more common than rounded ones. The finest range of Georgian fronts, mostly in deep red brick but with one, the tallest, in yellow bricks from Beaulieu, is on the north side towards the church, which closes the view along the street splendidly. It began as a chapel-of-ease to the nearby church at Boldre, and some medieval work survives in the eastern parts. The plain tower of white Purbeck stone, with a

later cupola, was built in 1670 and resembles that of Portsmouth Cathedral. The nave interior is surprising, with classical columns and galleries, looking something like a theatre – the result of successive alterations in the Georgian period. Amazingly, there was a pre-war plan to Gothicize it all. The street swings south of the church past a late seventeenth-century house called Monmouth House (there was much local support here for the rebel Duke, who is said to have been proclaimed king by the local people, in his absence, in the High Street). Looking back along the street, the descending view is closed by an obelisk rising among the trees across the estuary. This was erected in 1840 to commemorate Admiral Burrard Neale, M.P. for the borough, which had sent members since 1584, when the right was conferred by Queen Elizabeth, as at Haslemere. The Burrards, who lived in Walhampton House, usually controlled the voting up to the time of the first Reform Act, and even for a time after.

Newport

Isle of Wight

Newport, the chief town on the Isle of Wight, was founded about 1180 by Richard de Redvers, a member of the powerful family who were also earls of Devon, and became lords of the Isle in 1100. Their stronghold was Carisbrooke Castle, a Norman and later castle on the site of a Saxon fort. Carisbrooke, now a village on the outskirts of Newport, was the original chief place of the Island, but had the disadvantage of being nearly a mile from the head of the estuary of the River Medina where was the nearest quay – a specially important facility on an island. Newport was focused on that quay, with a complicated street pattern which largely survives. There is a rough grid of streets, including High Street running east-west, together with a diagonal street, Quay Street, leading north-eastwards to the quay. There were two market places, St Thomas' Square, originally rectangular, and St James' Square, which was a widening of one of the north-south streets. Although preserving its medieval layout, Newport has no medieval buildings, and very few from before the eighteenth century. Almost all that matter are Georgian and Victorian. They are nearly all classical – there are no Gothic fancies except the church – but immensely varied in detail and colouring. A few are of Island stone, some are stuccoed, but most are of brick. There is a great variety of clays suitable for brick-making on the Island, and this is reflected in Newport's buildings. Many are of dark red bricks; a large number are of rich

purplish-greys, with red-brick dressings; some are built of bricks which are individually mottled; many are of buffs and browns fashionable in the early nineteenth century. There is a fair number of bay windows; some are rounded, more are flat-fronted and canted, and a few are of a special local type with flat fronts and curved ends. Because of the shops along the main streets, a large proportion of the old façades survive on the upper storeys only.

A good place to start is St James' Square, a broadening street, focused on a florid memorial to Queen Victoria, lady of the Island. The dominating building is the County Club, built as the Literary Institute in 1810, to the design of John Nash – he, like the Queen later, had his retreat on the Island, at Cowes. It is one of Nash's most sober buildings, of white stone, with a pedimented upper storey projecting over the pavement on open arches. Round the corner is a long vista along High Street, with just enough minute changes on its medieval frontage to make it notably more interesting than an absolutely straight street would be. Its landmark, part of the way along, is the Guildhall, also by Nash, this time of stucco, its columns standing free in front of an open gallery, with another arched passage below. To it the loyal islanders added a Diamond Jubilee Tower in 1897, upsetting the balance of the building but providing a marvellous landmark in High Street. The Guildhall is at a complicated meeting of streets; Quay Street leads diagonally off, and opposite there is an opening into St Thomas' Square. What was originally a rectangular market place was encroached first by the original church

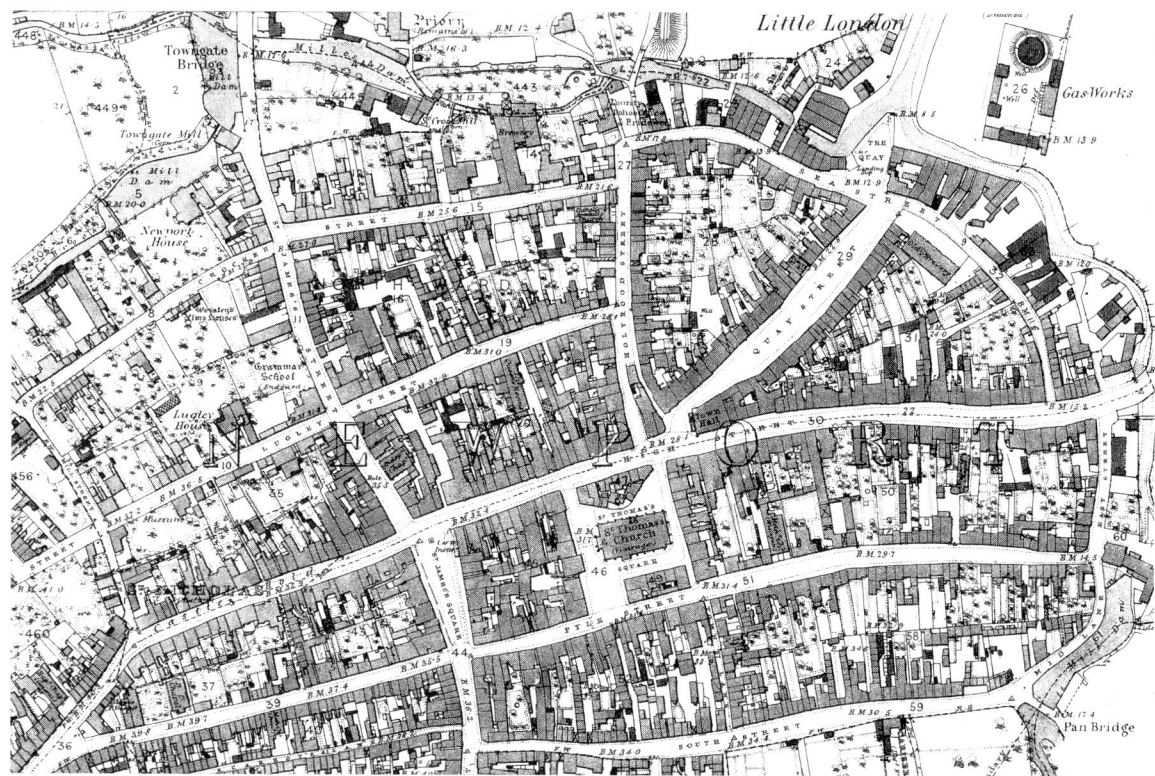

Map IV Newport, the chief town of the Isle of Wight, was founded in about 1180 by the lord of nearby Carisbrooke Castle. It has a loose grid of streets, with one leading diagonally to the quay on the River Medina, and two market places, the larger containing the church. The map is of 1863.

(a chapelry of Carisbrooke), dedicated to the newly martyred St Thomas, then by islanded blocks of buildings replacing market stalls. This has resulted in a small but subtle central space with lanes and passages leading off, dominated by the present St Thomas' – an assertive rebuilding of 1855 by the architect Samuel Daukes, of rough stone with finer dressings and a tall and very successful tower which culminates in a corner pinnacle. Enough of the buildings around are pleasantly small and simply classical to provide excellent foils to the church, as well as define the spaces effectively; the most distinctive is God's Providence House of 1701, with a later Georgian shop front and a shell-hooded doorway on a side lane. Quay Street is impressive but battered; it widens as it goes down to the quay, beside varied classical façades, many in purply brick. It used to end

with warehouses, but now there is an open view to the estuary. A few years ago this was a marvellous area with a series of warehouses, individually gabled, in various bricks and stones, abutting on to small inlets formed by tributary streams. Most have gone; those that remain are distinctive, with round-headed windows containing iron grills. There is – or was – a great deal more in other streets; despite erosion in the 1960s and 70s, Newport is still a town of great character, even if not appreciated enough.

Newport

Isle of Wight

Newtown is a town that came to nothing, except as an attractive hamlet. It was founded on a creek off the north coast of the Isle of Wight in 1255 by a Bishop of Winchester – one of the see's many ventures in town-building on their lands. Because of its potential strategic

importance, Edward I took it over as a royal borough in 1284. The French sacked it in 1377, and it never recovered; Newport proved a better site as the *entrepôt* for the Island. Traces of the layout survive – there were two long, slightly curving parallel streets, and two wider cross streets which contained the markets. Only parts of these are preserved as thoroughfares in the present scattered hamlet of partly stone-built houses; some of the others are represented by rough lanes. A small church with plaster-vaulted interior, by Augustus Livesay who designed Andover church (page 16), was built in 1835 on the site of the medieval church, which had fallen to ruin. More poignant is the little Georgian town hall of brick and stone, standing in a green space which had been one of the market places. The town had already nearly vanished when it was built – it was simply the base for the spectral borough corporation, and the place where the very few qualified voters cast their votes in this supremely rotten borough until the Reform Act of 1832.

Odiham

Hampshire

Odiham is an old market town which the railway missed, and which failed to grow in Victorian times. Only very recently have pressures for large-scale development started to build up in what is now a vulnerable corner of Hampshire. It has a long main street of varying width – broadening, narrowing, climbing. flattening – and the predominant material is, or was, Georgian brick of a warm rich red, but, unfortunately, too many of the brick façades have been painted over. Many of the buildings are, as usual, older behind the façades, and it seems that brick nogging (brick infilling within timber framework) began early here. The old main road (Odiham is now happily bypassed) enters the town from the west, where a house called the Priory is set back in large grounds; behind the Georgian frontispiece is a partly medieval building of flint, stone and early brick. It belonged to the medieval Chancellors of Salisbury Cathedral who were nominal rectors of Odiham, and were thereby entitled to the major part of the local tithes. The road narrows, running past garden walls shaded by trees, then broadens into a true town street. There are plenty of Georgian fronts of moderate scale, some with shops in the ground floors, others still domestic to street level, especially towards the east – these usually have classical doorcases or pillared

12 *Below*   **Odiham** is a former market town with a long and eventful main street. Georgian red brick predominates, but some of the frontages conceal older timber-framed buildings behind.

porches. There is a fine succession of the latter on the right as one goes down, followed by an impressive shell-hood on the door of an early Georgian house. Opposite this is a pair of houses with red-brick Georgian fronts, one with Venetian windows on the ground floor (12). No one would guess from the street that these houses are timber-framed and that the Georgian fronts were added, hiding the original first-floor jetty, nor that the modest plaster-fronted Nos. 28–30 further down were also jettied. In between, the White House of 1812 is detached and set back slightly behind a hedge – a pleasant variation to the otherwise nearly continuous frontages to the street. Further down, a green strip with a few trees lines the street on the right where it is widest, enlivening what might otherwise be a dull breadth of tarmac. The house behind the war memorial had a timber-framed hall, with gabled wing, altered and refronted in Georgian times.

Odiham has even more than its splendid main street. Church Lane leads south, past a house with a wood-framed medieval Gothic window, recently exposed, into The Bury – a fascinating little square with a good neo-Georgian house closing the view – beside it is a timber-framed house with its jetty intact. Southward is the church, a big medieval building altered in the seventeenth century, when the top of the tower with its decorative brickwork was built. The church is confusing inside. The north arcade, with three wide airy arches, probably dates from the fourteenth century, as do the arches from both aisles into the chapels, while the south arcade, with four narrower arches, is fifteenth century or later. (Pevsner, in the Hampshire volume of the *Buildings of England* series, suggested, surely wrongly, that the south arcade was older.) Two stained glass windows by the artist Patrick Reyntiens, who lived in the town, are in deep vivid colours, and the one representing the Tree of Jesse, with its blues and yel-

13 *Above*   **The Pest House, Odiham,** was built in the early 17th century to isolate sufferers from infectious diseases, in the hope of forestalling plagues.

lows, is haunting. Behind the church are seventeenth-century almshouses, with tall brick chimneys. Nearby is the Pest House of about the same date, a small building with a chimney, where infected people were confined during plagues, or as a precaution against epidemics – a piece of crude social provision that may once have been fairly common but of which this is a rare survival. Two landmarks on the southern edge of the town are octagonal cemetery chapels (for different denominations) of about 1860, with striking conical roofs supported internally by intricate timbering.

Petersfield

Hampshire

Petersfield is a market town *par excellence* – one of the few in the region with a rectangular market place which has not been infilled by permanent buildings, and where open markets are still held twice a week. The town seems to have been founded around the middle of the twelfth century by one of the powerful earls of Gloucester, whose estates were mainly in the west but who controlled the local manor – to a street plan still recognizable as regular, though subtle. The church stands to the south of the market place, with a fairly tame exterior that belies the magnificence of part of the interior. Its early history is a great puzzle; at first it was a mere dependency, or chapelry, to the parish church of nearby Buriton. Yet it was started very ambitiously, in about 1120, with a central crossing space which would have been comparable in style to, though smaller in scale than, that of Winchester Cathedral. The church was never finished to the first grand design; the rest of the building, where not re-stored, is more modest, though still impressive, later twelfth-century work. There is no documentary – only architectural – evidence for the origin of the church, but it may have been started by Robert Earl of Gloucester, bastard son of Henry I, and finished under his son

William who inherited the estates in 1147 and is usually thought to have founded the town. But if so, why start a church so ambitiously before there was a proper town?

In the middle of the square there is a splendid statue of William III, commissioned in 1757 (long after his death) by a local Whig resident whose family controlled the voting in what was then a rotten borough. Otherwise the interest of the square is accentuated at the corners, where streets lead off. At the north-west corner the outgoing road bends past a fine Georgian house with a stone doorcase, now a bank, and a timber-framed house with, unusually, flint 'nogging', or infilling in the timber framework. To the south-west is a recent group of buildings, including the public library, with a bizarre skyline, taking the corner with Sheep Street, which leads, past timber-framed houses, into The Spain. This was originally a second market place, rectangular in shape, which long since reverted to grass and now looks like a charming village green, intersected by roads, and surrounded by a variety of buildings, Georgian and earlier, some urbane, some rustic. The houses on the north side of The Spain are typical of a Hampshire town. One is of grey brick with red brick dressings; its neighbour is taller and more austere, with stuccoed front and classical doorcase, while at the north-east corner the scale is homelier – where the houses group round the corner into Sheep Street, the top of the church tower appearing behind. Southwards across the green – which has excessive traffic – there is a glimpse, between buildings, of the prominent rounded bluff of Butser Hill which, with its prehistoric earthworks, is the high point of the chalk downs on the Hampshire-Sussex border. However, Petersfield shows many other building materials related to the locality – flint from the chalk downs, hard rough sandstone from the Sussex border or, occasionally, malmstone, a soft chalky material. The stones and flints are often found in boundary walls, or on the sides of houses where the frontages are of brick, or plastered over. And of course there is timber-framing, sometimes seen only on the top floor above a brick- or stone-faced ground floor.

Petersfield's homely High Street leads east from the market place; it has a miscellany of still mainly Georgian fronts (occasionally older), mostly over shops, though one prominent Georgian house is still domestic to the ground, with a pillared porch. It leads to a crossroads; Dragon Street (south) and its continuation College Street (north) form, as they always have, part of the main route from Portsmouth to London – until the nearly imminent (at the time of writing) opening of a bypass. They have intermittent groups of attractive old buildings. No. 9 Dragon Street has a good early nine-

Map V **Petersfield** developed in the 12th century. It has an interesting plan, seen on this map of 1870, with a diagonal street linking two squares, one still the market place, the other (The Spain) now a pleasant green.

teenth century bowed shop front in a stuccoed front incised to resemble stonework, and Dragon House opposite has a typical Hampshire façade of blue-grey brick, with red brick round the window openings, added to an older building. In College Street the Red Lion is an old coaching inn, with broad bow windows on two façades which lit an assembly room upstairs, while the Old College is a splendid brick-fronted house in 1729, rather like some of the houses in Farnham – it accommodated Churcher's College, founded by an East India merchant, before the school moved to Victorian buildings further north.

Station Road leads to a mixed area of Petersfield, with a visual climax where two churches adjoin, in striking stylistic as well as sectarian contrast; the Methodist one has a prominent Gothic steeple of 1903 in dark flint profusely interspersed with red brick; the Catholic one of 1891 has a copper-covered dome. Both are seen, as an improbably exotic group, from trains on their way to Portsmouth. Chapel Street leads south to the vicinity of the station; it has a charming range of mid-Victorian gables above shops before it ends near the north-west corner of the Square.

Portsmouth

Hampshire

Portsmouth has its roots in the Middle Ages, though it did not become really important till Georgian times. Even in its natural state the harbour was ideal for anchorage. At first the main settlement was Portchester on the northern shore, where the Roman fort was turned into a Norman castle. About 1180 a small town was founded at the mouth of the harbour by John de Gisors, also lord of the manor of Titchfield. He rebelled against Richard I, who took over the youthful town and re-founded it as a royal borough in 1194. For a time the town did not fulfil its first promise and was overshadowed by Southampton. But the harbour was used from time to time for the assembly of ships against the French – who retaliated by sacking the town several times. The original town – the present Old Portsmouth – stands at one corner of Portsea Island, which is about four miles from north to south and is separated from the mainland at its northern end by a narrow creek.

Henry VII built a dry dock on the edge of the harbour, near where HMS *Victory* now is. Henry VIII built Southsea Castle on the coast outside the town, and nearby the *Mary Rose* sank in a skirmish with the French and Spanish in 1545. But for some time Portsmouth was less important as a naval base than the dockyards nearer to London – first Deptford, then Chatham. It started to develop significantly under Charles I, and still more after the Restoration. The dockyard expanded steadily through the eighteenth century and became, with those at Chatham and Devonport, one of the largest centres of employment in Britain, until overtaken by some of the great factories of the early nineteenth century. In the Napoleonic Wars Portsmouth really came into its own, and it is fitting that the city's historic centrepiece should be HMS *Victory*, berthed in a dock built three years before the battle of Trafalgar, and adjoining naval buildings of slightly earlier date. After the defeat of Napoleon there was a local lull, but in the 1840s the Dockyard expanded again, to provide for the age of steam. There was further expansion in the 1870s, culminating in the Edwardian era when huge battleships were built there. Meanwhile Portsmouth expanded from a town into a large city.

The more interesting parts of the city are covered, under these headings: *The Dockyard, The Defences, Old Portsmouth, The City Centre, Southsea.*

The Dockyard

The Dockyard has always been apart from the old and the modern centres of Portsmouth. It lay to the north of the old town from which it was separated, until the nineteenth century, by an inlet. Not until Georgian times did the area immediately adjoining the Dockyard become densely developed with streets – forming the district called Portsea. Nothing is left of Henry VII's dry dock, and the Great Stone Dock of 1691–8, the first of the recognizably modern docks, was completely altered in the 1760s and later, as No. 5 Dock. The earliest buildings, of which none survive, were of timber. From the 1760s there was continuous new building and replacement, at first using deep red local brick, then (after 1800) usually yellow brick. After 1840 there was a reversion to red brick, and buildings were erected on an even grander scale.

Visitors to HMS *Victory* pass the former Mast Pond with, at its end, the old No 6 Boat House of 1843, austerely classical outside, but with a magnificent iron-framed interior. Then follow three former storehouses,

14   Eighteen Gun Battery, Portsmouth, part of the old town's defences, remodelled in the mid-19th century from the 17th-century originals.

dating from 1782, 1776 and 1763 (going from south to north), to handsome classical designs, almost as if they were austere country houses; the inset passageways are part of the recent conservation scheme. Opposite the middle store is the end of the very long former Rope House, built in 1770 and burnt out six years later by Jack the Painter – a saboteur who symphathized with the rebelling American colonists, who had set fire to buildings elsewhere, and who was eventually hanged from the tallest mast available, in the Dockyard. Ropes ceased to be made there in 1868, and it was further adapted after the second world war. There are many other fine Georgian buildings out of sight of the usual visitors' route to the right, including what was originally the Royal Naval Academy, built in 1732 (the oldest building in the Dockyard), St Ann's church of 1786, and Admiralty House by Samuel Wyatt, the residence of the commander-in-chief. But the centrepiece is HMS *Victory*. She was built at Chatham in 1759–65, altered in 1800–3, and restored recently to the state in which she fought at Trafalgar. She is berthed in a stone-lined dock dating from 1801, one of a series then being built (incorporating the older Great Stone Dock) under the engineer Sir Samuel Bentham, brother of the political philosopher Jeremy Bentham, who had previously served in Catherine the Great's Russia and designed a new dockyard there. There is something particularly poignant about the great ship, built in timber following traditions of construction which did not change in essentials since the late Middle Ages, being berthed in a dock which was an early product of the age of technology. (Some will find it even more poignant that the remains of the *Mary Rose* are placed in an adjoining, similar, dock.) Bentham also built, in 1800, the Block Mills, unremarkable as a building but the scene of very important developments in technological history. Marc Isambard Brunel, originally a French naval officer who fled from the French Revolution and worked in New York for several years, came to England in 1801 – primarily, it is said, to marry Sophia Kingdom whom he met while still in France; it was a propitious marriage, for their son was the great Isambard Kingdom Brunel, born in Portsmouth in 1806 (in a house which no longer survives). Brunel worked under Bentham, in collaboration with another engineer, Henry Maudslay, in designing machinery, first installed in the Block Mills in 1802, for the making of pulley blocks. These, which took the strain of ropes in rigging, were of immense importance to the Navy and had previously been hand-made by an outside contractor. Brunel's machinery was steam-driven, and is said to have been the first in the world to mass-produce small components such as these. Some of the machinery is in the Science Museum in London; some is still *in situ*, but the Block Mills are not normally open to the public.

Despite this advance in the making of components, the Navy was at first very reluctant to adapt to steam propulsion or iron construction in the building of ships; there were, admittedly, technical difficulties in using coal-fired engines in long-distance vessels, which applied equally to civilian shipping. It was not until after 1860 that the Navy turned entirely to steam-driven, metal-built ships. But the Dockyard was greatly enlarged from the 1840s with buildings on a grand scale. The most magnificent is the one now called No. 2 Ship Shop, of 1848, designed by a Royal Engineer called Captain Sir William Denison. Outwardly it is one of the finest industrial buildings ever erected, with its round-arched openings and frieze of white Portland stone contrasting with the deep red brick of the walls. Unfortunately this, and other smaller but impressive Victorian buildings in similar style are in the part of the Dockyard seldom accessible to visitors.

Little is left of the Georgian dockyard workers' district of Portsea outside the gate – a scatter of bow-windowed houses, a pleasant church of 1754 (St George's), and an interesting early charitable school building of 1784, the former Beneficial School in King Street. Facing the Hard, near where the ferries to the Isle of Wight and Gosport depart, is a lively row of Victorian and Edwardian buildings in a variety of styles, many of them pubs.

Defences

In Portsmouth and Southampton together we can cover almost the whole history of defensive building up to the age of air attack – Southampton for its medieval walls (page 56), the Portsmouth area with Roman and medieval Portchester, the seventeenth- and eighteenth-century town defences, and the great Victorian forts. Portchester Castle, now within Portsmouth's suburban fringes, began as one of the Roman forts built in defence against Saxons and other barbarians, as at Pevensey. The outside walls of the fort survive almost entire, the highest Roman walls remaining above the ground in northern Europe. Into one corner were built a Norman keep, also well-preserved, and a small inner bailey with the remains of royal apartments, used on occasions when there were rallyings of ships in the harbour. Within the Roman enclosure is a very fine Norman church, also, just outside the fortress, the mainly Georgian village street of Portchester remains remark-ably unspoiled at its southern end.

Southsea Castle was one of several coastal forts built by Henry VIII from Kent to Cornwall, as at Deal; Yarmouth (page 77); Hurst near Lymington, and St Mawes; its low central keep looks remarkably like medieval pre-cursors. It was reconstructed in the seventeenth and, more thoroughly, the early nineteenth centuries, and is now a museum illustrating Portsmouth's defensive history. Nearby is the new purpose-built D-Day Museum.

The town of (Old) Portsmouth was defended only rudimentarily in the Middle Ages; it had nothing like the walls of Southampton. Medieval stone walls generally became obsolete with the development of cannon, and by the sixteenth century new forms of town defence were developed, including low, broad earthworks with projections, or bastions, at intervals, and moats. Both Berwick-on-Tweed and Portsmouth were fortified under Queen Elizabeth I in this way, and became the only towns in England, except possibly Plymouth, to be so defended. Because Britain, as an island, was free from continental-scale wars, the medieval walls of most other towns were not then kept in good repair, let alone improved (though some were hastily strengthened in the Civil War). This was in great contrast to the Continent with its almost endemic warfare, where most towns of any importance had to be elaborately fortified, following the new principles which were developed further by military engineers, of whom the most famous was the Frenchman, Vauban. Portsmouth, however, was of great strategic importance, and from 1665 its town defences were entirely remodelled, in the manner of Vauban, under the king's engineer-in-chief, Sir Bernard de Gomme. As modified in the eighteenth century they survived till 1870. They consisted of broad grassed ramparts with arrow-headed bastions at intervals, and a moat which contained further defensive works; beyond that was a series of outworks (called a glacis) which from the outside appeared as grassy banks. These at first surrounded only Old Portsmouth. In the 1770s they were extended northwards to provide continuous landward defence to the Dockyard and the adjoining district of Portsea. Almost all the ramparts were swept away in 1870–5, leaving only a short stretch, called the Long Curtain, near the sea in Old Portsmouth. This is a grassed embankment, ending in an arrow-headed bastion, with old guns reinstated; in front is a moat. It can give only a limited impression of what

15 Long Curtain, **Portsmouth**, the only surviving stretch of the old earthen ramparts.

the rest of the ramparts were like since, as it adjoined the open sea, it always lacked the elaborate outer works which existed elsewhere. (It must be added that Gosport was also fortified, more simply, to similar principles, and that parts of the earthworks survive there, page 26). North of the Long Curtain more conventional stone defences face the open sea, incorporating the original medieval Square and Round Towers (both drastically altered), and a remarkable range of gun emplacements called the Eighteen Gun Battery, built in the seventeenth century and enlarged in the nineteenth – including a two-tiered section projecting into the water. All these remaining defences have been transformed by the council into a complicated series of spaces and walkways open to the public, giving splendid views over the Solent. This is not entirely new, as it seems that the old earthen ramparts were often accessible to townspeople, even if unofficially, and provided a marvellous green amenity which it was tragic to lose.

Access to the fortified town was through a series of gates. To reach the Landport Gate, the principal entrance to Old Portsmouth, one had to pierce the outer defences and cross the moat twice before reaching the actual gate, a handsome classical structure rebuilt in 1760 with a strange octagonal turret. It survived the flattening of the ramparts on either side, the filling of the moat and the transformation of all else around, and now forms the impressive but forlorn entrance to the naval sports ground in St George's Road. Other gates survive re-sited, including the very fine classical Unicorn Gate, originally one of the entrances to Portsea, which is now an entrance to the Dockyard.

The earthen ramparts were built in response to the threat from simple cannon. A much later development was that of rifled artillery, firing explosive shells, which was introduced about 1860 – immediately trebling, or quadrupling, the range of guns from either land or sea. So a range of forts was built to defend the harbour from landward attack – it was seriously thought that the French might try and land on the Solent coast and attack Portsmouth from the side or rear. One line of forts was built across the Gosport peninsula, Fort Brockhurst among them (6) (page 27), and another line on Portsdown Hill, the long chalk ridge north of the harbour. Of these, Forts Widley and Nelson are now public showpieces. In some ways they were updated versions of medieval castles like Portchester on the plain below, with their massive outer ramparts of earth and brick, their 'defensible barracks' which in principle and appearance are remarkably like keeps, and their external moats which on Portsdown Hill have to be dry. They are among the most massive constructions ever to have been built of brick; some of the brick-vaulted chambers and tunnels look wonderfully impressive inside. There was much derision about these expensive and, as it turned out, unnecessary structures – and still more about the four forts on artificial islands which were built in the Solent – and they were given the name 'Palmerston's Follies' after the Prime Minister who advocated them.

Old Portsmouth

Although its ramparts were nearly all flattened in the 1870s, the old town of Portsmouth remains an entity, especially as much of the site of the ramparts is occupied by sports grounds. It was the main part of Portsmouth until well into the nineteenth century, when the present city centre developed and the old town became a backwater. It was heavily bombed; the gaps were filled by new private housing which at least respects the old street pattern, and the old town became a residential suburb. Most of the older houses that survived are now well looked after. John de Gisors, founder of the town, started the first church in the 1180s; the western parts were rebuilt after damage in the Civil War, and enlargement started after the church became the cathedral for a new diocese in 1927. But some of the earliest work survives at the east end, and very remarkable it is, unmistakably Gothic – among the earliest work in this style in the country. Pairs of arches are contained in wider arches – an arrangement unique in England except at Boxgrove Priory, east of Chichester. The additions after it became a cathedral, suspended in the second world war resulted in an awkward building, but a new west end by the architect Michael Drury has recently been built. Nearby is the Royal Garrison Church, founded in the early thirteenth century as a hospital for poor travellers and the infirm, with the aisled nave as the ward and the structural chancel as the chapel – much as in St Mary's Hospital, Chichester. It was restored by G.E. Street; the nave roof was lost by bombing, but the chancel is intact, with exquisite thirteenth-century vaulting.

There is little else of pre-Georgian date in the rough grid of streets which forms Old Portsmouth. Buckingham House, in High Street has a stuccoed Georgian front, but behind is the timber-framed house where the Duke of Buckingham, favourite of Charles I and inept minister of state, was murdered in 1628. He had arranged an unsuccessful expedition from Portsmouth to relieve the Huguenots at La Rochelle, and was preparing another. The house's owner was Captain John Mason, who had a distinguished record in promoting colonies, and was one of the founders of New Hampshire. Behind the cathedral, in Lombard Street, is a picturesque group with seventeenth-century Dutch-style gables. Otherwise there is a scatter of Georgian houses, often with the characteristic Portsmouth bow windows which have graceful shallow curves, each composed of three sash windows under a delicately detailed cornice. They contrast with the much more boldly rounded bows characteristic of Southampton.

The furthest part of Old Portsmouth is called Point, originally a shingle spit, behind and beyond the shoreside stone defences. It was notorious as the place where sailors came for comfort and excitement, especially when rowed ashore from ships anchored at Spithead. But it had other activities. Bathing took place off the shingly beach, and in 1754 a weatherboarded bath house was built, its lower level containing baths which were replenished by the tides. It is now called Quebec House (because it was later attached to the Quebec Hotel which accommodated passengers bound for North America) and is probably the oldest surviving structure in Britain built in association with sea bathing. Tower House nearby, north of the Tudor-to-Victorian Round Tower, was the home of W.L. Wyllie, painter of sea scenes, and one of the many artists of around the turn of the century whose work is probably due for reappraisal. Otherwise what is left of old Point is picturesque and well cared-for, with three pubs on the end of the spit which are familiar

16 Lombard Street, Old Portsmouth, one of the most attractive corners in the old town. The façades with the 'Dutch' gables were added to timber-framed houses in the 17th century, and have been altered many times since.

features from ships leaving the harbour. Finally, on the landward side of Old Portsmouth, are two remarkable buildings formerly barracks. Portsmouth had, till quite recently, a substantial garrison – the Army in readiness to defend the Navy. What is now Portsmouth Grammar School was built in the 1850s as a barracks, in a style characteristic of thirty years before, suggesting how conservative the army was on the eve of the Crimean War. Round the corner is another barrack block, now the City Museum, wildly different in its style, reminiscent of anything from a Scottish baronial hall to a Bavarian schloss. It is the only survivor of several barrack blocks which were built on part of the land freed by the removal of the ramparts.

The City Centre

By 1800 building spilled outside the ramparts of Old Portsmouth and the dockyard town of Portsea, especially along the winding road – later Commercial Road – which led from the Landport Gate of Old Portsmouth to the only bridge out of Portsea Island on to the mainland, about three miles to the north. This development soon consolidated, forming the district called Landport. The railway entered Portsmouth in 1847, terminating at first on the site of the present main station in the middle of the area – it was extended later, across Commercial Road to Portsmouth Harbour station. The presence of the railway encouraged the development of a shopping centre, which was well placed to serve the new housing areas which spread rapidly over the central parts of Portsea Island as the Dockyard expanded. By the end of the century it was the main shopping centre of greater Portsmouth, superseding the High Street of the old town (from which shops have since almost disappeared) – though there was rival shopping in Southsea. The status of the area as the main centre of Portsmouth was confirmed in 1886, when work started on the Guildhall, replacing a much more modest building in Old Portsmouth. It is the most imposing town or city hall south of London apart from the later Civic Centre in Southampton, and rivals the great town halls of the north, such as that at Leeds. The architect, William Hill, indeed came from Leeds, and designed the Guildhall on the same lines as an earlier one of his at Bolton, with a great portico and a tall turret. It was burnt out in the bombing, and when reconstructed within the shell lost some of its original skyline of subsidiary turrets.

Bombing devastated much of the city centre. The main shopping area north of the railway was unimaginatively rebuilt, although partial pedestrianization has resulted in improvement. South of the railway, where there were always fewer shops, more Victorian buildings survived. The Theatre Royal, with a lovely interior of 1900 by Frank Matcham, the leading theatre architect of the day, was nearly lost after the war but was saved through the persistence of local conservationists, who hope to bring it back into full use. It has a strange two-tiered frontispiece projecting over the pavement with an open-arched ground storey and a bar, recently re-opened, above. Next is a florid half-timbered pub of the type characteristic of Portsmouth around 1900, and on the other side a very impressive building designed by Alfred Waterhouse for the Prudential Assurance, in his characteristic style, rising with subtle elaboration to a fretted skyline, and faced with deep red brick and terracotta. Further south, a larger building of 1899 with turrets and florid gables, now called Charter House, was first built for the Pearl Assurance, and helps give scale and character to this part of the city.

For long the immediate surroundings of the Guildhall were in a dejected state. Plans were prepared in the 1960s by Lord Esher for a new civic square; they were partly carried out in the '70s by his successors, Teggin and Taylor. It is one of the more successful examples of civic design from the period. The square is just the right size to set off the Guildhall with its huge external staircase, and in the middle, at a carefully considered change in level, a statue of the aged Queen Victoria by Alfred Dury has been re-placed. On two sides are municipal buildings with glazed fronts, and at one corner is the very different, chunkier public library. The whole is an exercise in contrast and co-ordination. Originally there was to have been further re-development to the south (though retaining the Theatre Royal), but this part of the scheme has been modified. Behind the Guildhall is a very distinguished building of 1903–8, by the local architect G.E. Smith, built to house the Municipal College and the public library. It is exuberantly 'free baroque', with a decorative dome, and an undulating façade where the library was. Now it is all used by Portsmouth Polytechnic, into which the Municipal College has evolved. The Polytechnic has expanded over much of central Portsmouth, including some of the former military area; some – by no means all – of its recent buildings are impressive, notably the library designed by Ahrends, Burton and Koralek.

Southsea

Southsea is Portsmouth's seaside quarter, which began as a residential suburb rather than a resort. Its development started with a series of terraces, including Landport, Hampshire and King's Terraces, built in 1800–15 facing what were then the grassy outer earthworks of the ramparts. Mostly they were developed piecemeal, and they have been patchily altered since, but a few Georgian fronts survive, notably one in Landport Terrace with a two-tiered verandah. Behind were humbler streets, many of them damaged by bombing and redeveloped, but some are still colourful and attractive, notably Great Southsea Street and the winding Castle Road, dominated by a weird half-timbered clock tower of about 1900. In total contrast to these tight-knit streets is the early Victorian sylvan suburb further east, developed by Thomas Ellis Owen – a thrusting entrepreneur who was both speculative builder, trained architect and local politician. He was the son of a civilian engineer, Jacob Owen, who worked for the Army but also had a private architectural practice – his is the internally iron-framed Holy Trinity at Fareham (page 22). The younger Owen developed, with great flair, a large tract of what is now central Southsea. He catered for naval and military officers and their dependents, as well as for prosperous tradesmen and professional men who might previously have lived over, or near, their premises or practice in Old Portsmouth or Portsea. The movement of such people from old town centres to new residential districts was taking place all over the country at the time. Hitherto, such people would usually have moved into Georgian terraces, but from about the 1830s they increasingly sought detached (or semi-detached) houses in large gardens, as secluded as possible from each other and from the crowded and polluted inner districts, while remaining within carriage driving distance from the latter. This was the beginning of what were later called 'garden suburbs', such as were developing at the time round London, Birmingham and other big cities. Owen catered for this new demand, but for a time he also built terraces of the more traditional sort. 'Owen's Southsea' – this is the official title of a Conservation Area – has suffered from sporadic rebuildings, alterations and changes of use, but much of its sylvan, secluded character survives. His earliest houses are terraces of 1837–40 on the corner of Kent and Sussex Roads, set back behind well-planted gardens. The later Sussex Terrace, reached by a deliberately double-twisted road, has strange Moorish-like porches. All around are, or were (some have been replaced) stuccoed villas in versions of Gothic or Italian themes. St Jude's church with its striking spire was built by Owen as a centrepiece for the area. To the south, Portland Terrace of 1846, was a last grand design by Owen in the late Regency tradition. The most attractive piece of Owen's suburban scenery, The Vale, lies to the east of what is now the busy Palmerston Road shopping centre; it is a narrow twisting lane laid out in about 1850, from which gabled villas are glimpsed amid well-grown greenery, above brick and stone garden walls.

Portsmouth grew hugely from the mid-nineteenth century. Much of the growth was in the form of tight-knit terrace houses, some of which have lively and varied details in doorways and bay windows. The large villas in parts of Southsea – Waverley and St Andrew's Roads for instance – are often fanciful in their shapes and styles. Public houses are great features of the city with their lively exteriors, often showing half-timbering, colourful glazed tiling or both. Many schools were built after the Education Act of 1870; these often have elaborate skylines related to the large and tall windows on which educationalists of the time insisted. Schools and public houses, sometimes designed by the same local architects (notably the versatile A.E. Cogswell), provided the main visual landmarks amidst the miles of terraces, together with churches. Of the later churches in Portsmouth, mention must be made of the former St Agatha's, long secularized and now being refurbished, including its remarkable internal decoration in sgraffito (a form of plasterwork) by the still under-appreciated artist Heywood Sumner, who lived in later life (when he practised as an archaeologist) in a house he designed on the edge of the New Forest.

Reigate

Surrey

Reigate is not memorable for buildings or townscapes, but is pleasant none the less. It is built on hummocky sandstone hills, under the much bolder slope of the chalk downs, whence came its famous stone. Open spaces, both within and around the town, are among its most distinctive features. One is the site of the castle, built by the militant-pious Warenne dynasty, who first obtained the overlordship, like that of Lewes, after the Conquest. Nothing solid is left of the castle, save a charming 'Gothick' arch built out of salvaged stonework in 1777, but the grounds are a pleasing warren of municipal planting. The castle hill is about as high as the rooftops of High Street below, down to which a steep path descends. The street has a pleasant shape, gently curving and widening at both ends, with just enough interesting buildings: a few of them are

Georgian or earlier, but some of the most prominent, as so often in Surrey, are Victorian with busy and prominent skylines; the dead hand of redevelopment has so far blighted High Street only a little. The heart of the town is the delightful Old Town Hall of 1729, in Georgian red brick, with a rounded end, islanded in the wide eastern end of High Street. North of it is the town's most surprising feature, a road tunnel, under the castle hill, built in 1824 to ease the route for coaches from London to Brighton, but now closed to traffic. At the other end of High Street several streets meet at a confusing junction, with some pleasant buildings but no visual coherence. But it is worth going along West Street even though, like High Street, it is plagued with traffic – Reigate has not yet sorted out the problem of its through traffic. Towards its far end a house of 1786 stands on a wedge-shaped site, with two public fronts, a pleasant prologue or epilogue to the centre of the town.

Reigate's two finest buildings are away from the town centre. The Priory, on the site of a monastery founded by the Warennes, was the home of Lord Howard of Effingham, commander at the time of the Armada. Now it has a demure stuccoed Georgian main front, facing what is now a public park; inside there are a superb Tudor fireplace and an early Georgian staircase. The church is well to the east of the centre, indicating that the medieval castle-town developed away from the site of the original village, where the church remained. It is a big regular building, much restored, but distinctive outside for its walls of white stone – the chalky stone quarried from the neighbouring hills which was much used in London in the Middle Ages; Westminster Abbey was largely built of it. Unfortunately it does not usually weather well (which is why Westminster Abbey has had to be entirely refaced externally in different stones), but lends itself to fine carving and can last indefinitely internally – as the Abbey interior shows. But in Reigate church much of the internal stonework has been renewed, including the very fine late twelfth-century arcades – which were carefully and accurately reconstructed by the second George Gilbert Scott in 1877–81. The undulations to the south-east of the town are covered by well-to-do houses, Victorian and early twentieth-century. They rise to Redhill Common, a surprisingly half-wild tract which extends into the more open Earlswood Common on high ground overlooking the Weald. Here is the parish church of St John, Redhill, originally early nineteenth century but reconstructed by the great J.L. Pearson in 1889–95; his is the beautiful slender spire, soaring above the grassy slopes. The town of Redhill, though joined municipally to Reigate, has its own centre which developed round the station on the Brighton line, originally opened in 1841. For long the town was determinedly Victorian, but a shopping precinct called Warwick Quadrant now catches the eye, with round-framed glazed roofs in romantic reminiscence of building like the Crystal Palace, following a current architectural fashion.

Ringwood

Hampshire

Ringwood is the old market town of the Avon valley, a fertile strip up to two miles wide between the wild heaths of the New Forest to the east, and once equally deserted heathlands to the west, the latter now extensively sprawled over by development inland from Bournemouth. The old town centre keeps its character, partly through the effects of conservation and listed building legislation. A series of winding, branching streets runs roughly south to north, widening into the market place, which is cut off at its northern end by the roaring A31 – a tight bypass indeed. The market place should be visited on Wednesdays when it is crowded with stalls – a scene which with a little imagination could conjure up Hardy's Wessex; Dorset is not far away. There are Georgian buildings in prominent places, including the one-time Town Hall (nos. 18–20), sadly empty at the time of writing, and a fine double-bowed shop front on the opposite side. The church, prominently placed, is a complete rebuilding of 1853–5 by F. & H. Francis of London, architects also of Italianate office blocks in the City. Although it is sometimes said to have been in part a replica of the older church, the present interior is probably grander than the old one was; the severely impressive range of lancet windows in the chancel may have had precedent.

West Street leads off the market place, also cut off by the bypass, though it was once the main route out of the town across the Avon – the three-arched late Georgian bridge can be seen from an attractive little park through which flows one of the river's side streams. But Ringwood's most special building is behind the eastern side of the market place, in an area of former backland which has been laid out for car parks and bus station, bordered by shops. This is the Old Meeting, a simple chapel built in 1727 for a Presbyterian congregation, but used from the nineteenth century until the 1970s by the Unitarians. It retains a Nonconformist interior of the eighteenth century, with its pews, gallery, pulpit and other features very little altered – a rarity anywhere and unique in Hampshire. However, it is normally closed, with no indication of when and how to gain access.

Keen explorers of towns might walk along the narrow High Street, attractive through its varied upper stories, then its long continuation Christchurch Road. At the beginning of the latter road is the town's best former house, Greyfriars, early Georgian with pediment, pilasters and keystones over the windows – now a community centre. Past a spiky Congregational Church of 1866 by Thomas Hellyer of Ryde, then an occasional fine Georgian house and many pleasant smaller ones, a few of them thatched, one reaches the corner where Coxstone Lane leads off to the right. This short road with sharp bends has a group of thatched cottages worthy of the best picture postcards. It emerges on to a pleasant grassy common, from which there are several ways back to the High Street.

Romsey
Hampshire

Romsey has always been dominated by its abbey – as a nunnery before the Reformation, and as a very large parish church since. The nunnery was founded by 907 at the latest. It has its own saint, Ethelfleda, an abbess; another abbess was sister of St Margaret, queen of Scotland, and the latter's daughter Matilda, later queen of Henry I, was educated there. The church was rebuilt on a grand scale from about 1120 and survives almost intact – probably the finest Norman building in England apart from Durham Cathedral. Its Romanesque qualities are brought out superbly by the creamy grey stone – from Binstead in the Isle of Wight, of which the main parts of Winchester Cathedral are built – although the later parts to the west, where the Gothic style begins to take over, are of the more greeny Chilmark stone from Wiltshire, of which Salisbury Cathedral is built. In the Middle Ages the townspeople worshipped in a small outer aisle, since demolished, and in part of the north transept, but at the Dissolution they bought the whole church at its 'scrap value' of £100 (the estimated resale price of the materials), to their eternal credit. Romsey has grown recently and its eastern approach has always been scrappy. But the intricate historic centre now looks well conserved. It was not always so; until fairly recently some of the old streets were shabby, with gaps in the frontages. In the last few years such gaps have been filled, re-creating the former street lines, and old houses have been successfully repaired or rehabilitated.

The centre of the town is the informal Market Place, part of an originally larger, roughly triangular space which, as so often, was reduced in size by early encroachments. These are represented today by the irregular block which includes the Victorian former Corn Exchange – converted into a bank early this century when the windows were altered – and another building, also a bank, with an impressive curved frontage faced with mathematical tiles, resembling bricks.

Georgian red brick is the dominant material around the Market Place, especially on the series of three-storeyed buildings on the western side, which back on to the Abbey (17). Here and there are signs of older timber-framing, for instance in the courtyard of the White Horse, behind its painted Georgian façade.

Streets lead casually out of corners of the Market Place in three directions. The busiest is The Hundred leading east, narrow and irregular, with many of the town's shops. Other streets branch from it, the most remarkable of which is Palmerston Street, opening off with a bold curve southwards. This has several Georgian cottages with simple doorcases and a few larger houses of similar date, but its main landmark is the Manor House, now a restaurant, a timber-framed building with three steep gables above jettied upper storeys. The part under the northern gable has plastering between the timbers and probably dates from the fifteenth century. The rest of the building may be about a century later and has brickwork (brick nogging) within the timber framework – if this is original, it is a notably early example of this practice.

The street leading north out of the Market Place, Church Street, passes the approach to the Abbey on one side and, on the other, a narrow alley, easily missed, leading to Romsey's second most remarkable building, the so-called King John's House. This was a mid-thirteenth century house (slightly later than its name suggests) of stone and flint, which had been 'lost' through being altered and subdivided, until it was rediscovered in 1927; it has subsequently been well-, but not over-, restored, retaining and revealing what survived of the original. There is one main room on the first floor (later partitions have been removed), showing much of the medieval roof, parts of the original windows with some rich detail, and, most interestingly, the remains of graffiti incised in plaster on parts of the walls. These have been plausibly dated to the early fourteenth century because of heraldic evidence and,

17 **Market Place, Romsey,** with the Abbey rising behind; the statue is to Lord Palmerston, who lived in neighbouring Broadlands.

especially, a roughly drawn royal head with crown, which has been recognized as resembling the head of Edward I on surviving coinage of 1302–10. It is known that Edward visited Romsey in 1306 and the devices may have been scraped by members of his retinue lodging here. What precisely was the building's status we do not know. It has a tiny timber-framed Tudor wing, and the whole is opened regularly.

Church Street continues, past restored old buildings and new ones filling former gaps, to the one-time Strong's Brewery, now being converted or redeveloped A five-storey brewery 'tower' dating from 1929 has been converted to offices and looks like a post-modern slab block. Past Horsefair, with more restored old houses, and right into Cherville Street. This looks at first an unprepossessing thoroughfare because of fairly recent redevelopment, on a set-back line, at its southern end – indicating what was intended a few years ago further along the street. Fortunately the Romsey and District Preservation Trust was formed and, after successfully opposing demolition of some of the houses in the street at an inquiry, bought several of them and restored them. They are mostly fairly simple Georgian or early Victorian though one or two are older behind their façades. As a result Cherville Street – which once formed the principal approach to Romsey from the north, with the Abbey framed between its frontages – has been rescued and made more attractive than before,

instead of being turned into a widened, dull thoroughfare.

The Abbey has a definite precinct, though not so called. It is entered from the Market Place through a flint-faced Gothic gateway, improbably built in conjunction with the adjoining Congregational Church in 1888. A row of pleasant Georgian-looking houses occupies the site of, and incorporates parts of, some of the conventual buildings to the south of the Abbey. A path continues west, increasingly rural, crossing successive branches and sidestreams of the River Test, to pass an old mill and eventually to reach a classical bridge – Middle Bridge, originally of 1783, rebuilt in replica – over the main stream of the Test. Here one looks into the grounds of Broadlands, the great Georgian and earlier house which was the home of Lord Palmerston (who is commemorated by a statue in the Market Place), and more recently of Lord Mountbatten. One can return into the town by the long and versatile Middlebridge Street, with a stream on one side, and a variety of Georgian and earlier cottages and houses, many recently refurbished, then along Bell Street, narrower and with taller houses, which leads into the Market Place.

Ryde

Isle of Wight

Ryde, one of the two biggest towns on the Isle of Wight, is a creation of the nineteenth century; two previous hamlets were insignificant. The first pier was opened in 1814, to half the length of the present one, and a regular service of steamboats from Portsmouth started in 1825; from then development was rapid. The seafront is not specially notable; the interesting parts of Ryde are along the streets on the steadily rising slope to the south. The finest building is the Royal Victoria Arcade of 1835–6, designed by William Westmacott and named after Victoria as Princess; she stayed at about that time in Norris Castle near Cowes. The entrance front on Union Street is altered, but the classical interior is superb, though small, with its panelled-ceilinged passageway leading to a circular domed space. It must be the best pre-Victorian (though only just) arcade in England outside London. Behind is Brigstocke Terrace, the only one of its kind in Ryde, a monumental composition of 1833 by John Sanderson, with a rhythmically projecting and receding front; for long in a bad state, it was rehabilitated a few years ago. Not far away is the Town Hall, also by Sanderson, with a stucco and yellow brick exterior, built in 1834 – indicating how rapidly Ryde had acquired town status, even though it did not yet have a council. The tall thin clock tower was added in 1864. As often in early town halls the ground floor was intended for marketing, as was the colonnaded building to the east. Houses were built individually or in small groups, and there are still many stuccoed examples of about 1815 to 1840, some with bold bows, in the streets east and west of the town centre. From the 1840s the villas followed Victorian stylistic fashions, and many were built in the varied local stones. Ryde has two notable churches; All Saints (1868–72) is an ambitious work of Sir Gilbert Scott with a spire said to have been modelled on that of St Mary's at Oxford; it is a landmark from and across the Solent. St Michael's at Swanmore (1861–3), a remote suburb to the south-west, has a fantastic interior in High Victorian Gothic, with polychrome brickwork in buff, red and black.

Ryde's western suburb, Binstead, is interesting not for itself but because it was the site of famous limestone quarries. Stone from here was used by the Romans – for instance in the walls of their fort at Portchester near Portsmouth. Bishop Walkelin used the finest variety to build the Norman Winchester Cathedral, as did William of Wykeham for his remodelling three hundred years later. Quarr Abbey nearby, named from the quarries, was founded in 1131. The stone was found in several varieties, called variously, and not very consistently, Binstead stone, Quarr stone or, for no obvious reason, Bembridge stone. The best is hard and creamy, as used at Winchester and in Romsey Abbey; other layers produced rough stone often with a brownish mottled texture, seen in the Southampton city walls and in numerous parish churches on the mainland. The best deposits were exhausted centuries ago, and some of the early quarry sites are now covered in woods.

Southampton

Hampshire

18 *Opposite* **Bugle Street, Southampton,** the city's best old street; in the background are the many-gabled Tudor House with a restored front of *c.*1500 and the 1963 flats on the site of the castle keep.

Southampton first became a major port around 700–850 when, as *Hamwic* or *Hamtun* it had a thriving trade with northern Europe from the Seine to the Rhine. Archaeologists have revealed a pattern of regular streets, indicating that it was one of the largest English settlements at a period when few other places were recognizable as towns. *Hamtunscir* (Hampshire) was recorded in 757 – the first known reference to a county named after a town. This early town lay near the present St Mary's church (on the site of the first Saxon church) adjoining the Itchen estuary. It declined after about 850, when the activities of the Vikings affected the whole pattern of trade on which it depended. At about that time development started on a site to the west, adjoining the River Test, from which the modern city grew. The re-sited town, already called *Suthamtun* (to distinguish it from *Northamtun*), was important at the time of the Norman Conquest. A castle was built by the Test shore, and colonists from Normandy settled in the area around St Michael's and French Street. When Winchester was the royal residence, and Normandy politically linked with England, Southampton was a vital place of transit, and it developed trade further along the European coasts. By the end of the twelfth century rich merchants built stone houses, parts of which survive,

along and near the waterfront. After the breaking of English ties with Normandy, trade continued with western France, as well as Flanders and Spain. Wine was imported, together with dyestuffs, vegetable oil and fruits; wool and cloth were exported. Southampton was deeply involved with the French wars. Edward III's forces embarked there for the campaign which culminated at Crécy, as did Henry V's before Agincourt. But the French devastated the town in 1338, and it took decades to recover. After that, strong walls were built along the waterfront, and were effective in repelling another French attack in 1377, at a time when Portsmouth, Yarmouth, Newtown (Isle of Wight) and other towns were sacked.

Southampton reached another of its peaks of prosperity in the fifteenth century. Traders from Venice and Genoa made it one of their chief ports of call in northern Europe, bringing spices, silks, dyestuffs and other expensive cargoes in exchange for wool and woven cloth. The imported goods were mostly carried overland to London; the wool and cloth came from a wide hinterland including Wiltshire and even the Cotswolds; Salisbury merchants traded through the port. But in the sixteenth century there was a decline. The Italian ships ceased to call. More overseas trade, including that in West Country cloth, became concentrated on London. Southampton was reduced to a modest Channel port competing with places like Weymouth and Poole, though the connection with Portugal remained. There were inflows of Walloon (French-speaking) refugees from the Low Countries in the 1560s, and of Huguenots a century later.

Southampton became a Georgian resort. A spring with medicinal qualities was exploited, and the Prince of Wales visited the town in 1750. Baths, re-plenished with sea water, and assembly rooms were built by the shore. But Southampton never seriously rivalled Brighton. Rather it became a favoured place for residence and retirement. Jane Austen lived in the town from 1806 to 1809 (her house no longer exists); she described the balls held in the assembly room at the Dolphin inn.

Southampton's trade braced up a little in the early nineteenth century – it became again a place of military assembly during the wars. But the modern city really dates from 1840, when the railway from London was opened – the first long-distance line out of London except that to Birmingham. Two years later the first dock was opened. From then Southampton grew into a world port – Peninsular and Oriental, Royal Mail and what became Union Castle were some of the shipping lines making it their base in Victorian times. The London and South-Western railway company bought the docks in 1892 and developed them with flair. In 1907 the White Star Line made Southampton, instead of Liverpool, the main port for its transatlantic liners (including the *Titanic*); the Cunard company followed suit in 1919. The main reason for preferring Southampton was that it had open quays which – because of the Solent's double tides – were accessible to the biggest ships most of the time. Southampton's peak as a passenger port was reached in the 1930s. The railway company – then the Southern – constructed enormous new docks on reclaimed land, and the town responded by building what was probably the most ambitious inter-war group of civic buildings in Britain.

In the two world wars Southampton was of crucial importance – in both as a place of embarkation, and in the second because it had become the centre of an inventive aircraft industry, which included among its products the Spitfire fighter plane. Bombing devastated the shopping centre, and much of the riverside areas, including the Spitfire factory (but not before production had been transferred elsewhere). Rebuilding in the 1950s was sadly uninspiring; in the 1960s planners followed fashionable trends with tall blocks and ring roads. The university, rooted in a pre-1914 college, expanded to interesting overall effect. Present-day Southampton is a strangely mixed city – bland and featureless in the shopping centre; dramatically historic in the long battered but now sympathetically conserved old town; leafy in its ancient open spaces converted into parks (in the city centre) or kept half-wild (the Common); delightful in the inter-war suburbs designed by Herbert Collins. But, despite all the subsequent development, it is still the remains of the medieval town that impress most.

The best place to start an exploration of Southampton is the Bargate. This was the north gate of the town; now it is at the southern end of the main shopping centre. Right up to the 1930s buildings hemmed it in and vehicles went through; since then it has stood in a traffic circus. The core – an arch

19 High Street, Southampton; the appalling post-war buildings on the left contrast with those on the right, including the Dolphin of 1775 with, reputedly, the largest bow windows in England; in the background is the restored south front of the Bargate.

20 *Right*   **City Wall, Southampton.** The 14th-century arcade was added in front of a 12th-century merchant's house, the windows of which can be seen.

embedded in the gateway – is late Norman. Two large half-round towers were added on the north side in the thirteenth century. The south façade was thoroughly restored in 1864, but the splendid north façade remains largely as it was built in the late fourteenth century, in front of the original gate and rounded towers. Records show that in 1378 Henry Yevele, the royal architect, and William of Wynford, Wykeham's architect at Winchester, were commissioned to find masons for work on the Southampton defences. As the north front is in Wynford's style, it is quite possible that he was the designer, just as Yevele may have designed the Westgate at Canterbury. Most of the rough hard stone of which the Bargate and the walls are built – grey with rusty patches – came from the Binstead quarries on the Isle of Wight (page 52).

It is not far from the Bargate, along the intermittent line of the northern city wall, to the jagged Arundel Tower at a corner of the walled town and, then, round the corner, to a dramatic stretch of wall which once faced open water, built in the fourteenth century against what had been a low cliff – thus strictly a retaining wall. It was made still more impressive when the half-round Catchcold Tower with its machicolated parapet was added in the fifteenth century, and it now holds its own, looking like a huge piece of stage scenery, despite the busy road in front and the 1960s towers to the north. Back to the Bargate, and to High Street leading south. Photographs from early this century ahow that this street had irregular grandeur, its slightly veering alignment punctuated by bay windows and culminated by churches. Bombing was bad, and rebuilding dreadful. But something remains of the old quality. Lloyds Bank of 1927 by Horace Field puts the later buildings to shame. It stands between two coaching inns, the Star with a late Georgian stuccoed front, and the Dolphin of 1775 with two splendid ranges of bow windows, said to be the largest of their kind. Opposite the fourteenth-century tower of Holy Rood church, the ruins of which are maintained as a seamen's memorial, is a vigorous Victorian bank, formerly the National Provincial, designed, like the company's old headquarters in Bishopsgate, London, by the versatile John Gibson.

Holy Rood used to have a spire, lost in the war, which counterpoised that of St Michael's, further west. This, rebuilt and heightened in the nineteenth century as a landmark for shipping, rises from an older tower, supported internally by four austere arches, built soon after the Norman Conquest or even just before. The church faces St Michael's Square, once the fish market, and opposite is Tudor House, given to the town, after being thoroughly restored, as a museum in 1911. The front part was built about 1500 by Sir John Dawtrey of Petworth when he was customs collecter. Although the external timber details were mostly renewed, old photographs show that the form of the frontage is largely original (except the ground floor), though the half-timbering was then plastered over; it may have originally been exposed. The great hall and a long wing behind are basically older. The garden, extending towards the city wall, has lately been laid out to a Tudor design by Sylvia Landsberg. The final, great, surprise for a visitor is the stone shell of a late Norman merchant's house at the end of the garden, its lower storey well below garden level. The roof and intermediate floor have gone, but a stone fireplace remains *in situ* at first-floor level – one of the earliest of its kind in existence. Another fireplace of similar date, with a stone chimney shaft, nearly unique, was re-erected here from a bomb-damaged house elsewhere. The shoreside frontage to the Norman house was incorporated into the city wall in the fourteenth century, in a way which is described later.

Bugle Street, now the city's best historic street, leads south from Tudor House, with medieval to modern houses making an attractive mixture. Today

21 Below **Westgate and Merchants' Hall, Southampton.** The Westgate gave access to the medieval quay; the 15th-century Merchants' Hall was re-erected here in the 17th century.

it is one of the most sought-after places to live in the city, but in Victorian times it adjoined one of the worst slum areas. Historic but hopelessly insanitary houses in nearby Simnel Street were cleared away by a progressive council in the 1890s, and replaced by council dwellings – which were themselves demolished a few years ago. New red-brick many-gabled housing in the jittery style of the 1980s has replaced them, self-consciously picturesque and particularly effective where it faces the city wall. But one small block of 1890s council housing remains, surmounting a fine vaulted medieval undercroft. The tall tower block to the north, dating from 1963, stands on the site of the castle keep. It is now *de rigueur* to condemn all high-rise housing, but this is a sophisticated design, not brutal – the architect was Eric Lyons, better known for his cosy two-storey housing. Down Simnel Street to the city wall again. The busy road outside the wall runs over the site of the original shore-line and the medieval West Quay, where most of the early shipping was moored. The Georgian assembly rooms, long vanished, stood nearby, as did the first baths – the striking swimming baths of 1962 by Lewis Berger, then city architect, stand near their site. This stretch of city wall is wonderfully impressive. When it was built along the hitherto undefended waterfront after the French raid of 1338, the frontages of some of the stone-built shoreside houses, which had been damaged in the raid, were incorporated in the defences. An arcade of blind arches was built in front of them, broad enough to accommodate a walkway on top, with spaces at the heads of the arches for molten lead or missiles to be dropped on attackers. The most exciting stretch is where the outer wall of the Norman house, already described from Tudor House garden, appears behind the arcade, with double round-headed windows – long blocked, now re-opened. But the archway which originally gave access from the house to the quay remains as it was blocked in the fourteenth century, with keyhole-shaped slits designed to take small primitive guns. This may be the oldest extant example of defensive work designed for gun warfare – which eventually made town walls like this obsolete (page 42).

Further on is the Westgate, fairly modest considering it opened on to the principal quay. The timber-framed building just inside the gate, confusingly called the 'Tudor Merchants' Hall', originally stood in St Michael's Square and was used by cloth merchants. In 1634 it was demolished and re-erected here. On the old site the ground floor was open-sided, as in the re-sited market hall of Titchfield (page 64), but it was enclosed on re-erection. The city wall continues a little further – partly a Victorian rebuilding on this stretch – and then ends, the next stretch having been lost. A column commemorates the sailing of the Pilgrim Fathers in the *Mayflower* and *Speedwell* in 1620. The *Speedwell* proved unseaworthy, and it was the *Mayflower* alone which finally left Plymouth. This unintended departure from Plymouth is now far better known than the original embarkation at Southampton.

There are several interesting buildings in the only area where the old town faces open water – between the Victorian Eastern Docks and the inter-war Western Docks. The Wool House, built about 1400 as a warehouse, is now a maritime museum. One can stand, under the splendid original roof, amid models of old ships, and look out of the window at a modern liner in port. Next to the Wool House, in effective contrast, is the elaborately stuccoed

22 Yacht Club and Wool House, Southampton. The former Yacht Club, 1846, indicates how early fashionable yachting began in the Solent; the medieval Wool House is now a museum.

Italianate façade of what was originally the Royal Southern Yacht Club, built in 1846 when Southampton itself was the hub of fashionable sailing in the Solent, now centred on Cowes. A different note is struck by the sugary entrance to the former Royal Pier, opened in 1833 for the new steamships to France and the Isle of Wight – predating all piers built for pleasure. (Brighton Chain Pier was ten years older, but it too was primarily for berthing.) Later it did develop for pleasure, hence the sugary entrance, which was built in the 1920s, and is likely to be all that remains, as the rest is doomed. Behind a tall block of warehouses facing the front, converted into flats, is another medieval survival – the ruin of a merchant's house of just before 1200, called Canute's Palace by a romantic historian, because Southampton was supposedly the place where he rebuked his courtiers. Yet another fascinating group of buildings lies to the east. The centrepiece is God's House down narrow Winkle Street, founded about 1185 as a hospice for poor travellers and others – an earlier counterpart of the hospital at Portsmouth (page 44) and the Maison Dieu at Dover. There is nothing left of the medieval buildings except the restored chapel of St Julian, which retains its original fine chancel arch. Its great interest is that services were held there for Walloon and later Huguenot refugees, their descendants, and other French speakers from Tudor times till 1939; even now there is an annual service according to the Anglican prayer book in French. God's House gives its name to the adjoining Gate at the south-east corner of the town, one of the three town gates to survive, and to the impressive God's House Tower, built as a projection from the town walls in the fifteenth century.

Eastward is an area which derives its character from the development of the modern port. The centrepiece is the former Terminus Station, preserving the main classical block of Sir William Tite's station of 1839–40, closed a few years ago (the trains go by another route). Both the station and the nearby streets, developed at the same time, are more Georgian than early Victorian. Oxford Street takes a bend with a series of bow-windowed houses – almost semicircular in the Southampton tradition – making a marvellous interplay of curves. There is another range of bows in Bernard Street to the north, and there are more in Queen's Terrace facing the park. These streets were dilapidated a few years ago; recently the whole area has been uplifted. Adjoining the old station is the former South-Western Hotel, now offices, taking a bold corner opposite the entrance to the docks – an impressive Victorian building of 1867 reminiscent of a French château, rising to a complex roof with porthole windows in the attic. Here people stayed before joining and after leaving liners. Around 1920 an extension, contrastingly classical in Portland stone, was built for the extra clientèle following the transfer of Cunard liners to Southampton. The road past the entrance to the docks is called Canute Road – perhaps a Victorian engineers' joke, since it follows the old shoreline, those engineers having succeeded in doing what Canute could not do; to cause the sea to recede. A little way along, and up a side street, is the Hall of Aviation, an imaginative addition to Southampton's many museums, commemorating the area's critical role in the early development of aircraft.

The post-war shopping centre, Above Bar, is almost all dispiriting except for the surviving side of Regency Portland Street leading off, the bordering parks, and one good 1960s building with jutting glazed façades on a corner, making a prelude to the Civic Centre. This product of municipal pride in the 1930s, claimed to be the first to use the rather frigid title – combining council offices, Guildhall, law courts, library and art gallery – is a successful spread-out composition in modernized classical style, culminating in a tall tapering tower, which chimes every four hours the tune of *O God our help in ages past*. The words of the hymn (not the tune) were written by Isaac Watts, the greatest English hymn-writer, not excepting Charles Wesley. He lived as a youth in Southampton in the late seventeenth century, the son of a member of the Independent (later Congregational) church. He is commemorated in Watts Park – one of the series of medieval common fields turned into Victorian parks – by a life-size statue, with finely detailed relief panels illustrating his life. Clearly this was by a good sculptor – he was the almost unknown Richard Cockle Lucas, who lived a reclusive life in nearby Chilworth; almost the only other significant work by him is the even better statue of Dr Johnson in the market place at Lichfield. Nearby is Lutyens' impressive Cenotaph, commemorating those who died in the first world war. Opposite is another poignant memorial, in memory of the ship's engineers who went down with the *Titanic*.

23 **South-Western House, Southampton**, built as a hotel in 1867 for people joining or leaving liners; the tall extension was added *c.*1920 when Cunard transferred their transatlantic liners to Southampton.

Further north is Southampton's 'Regency' area, developed from about 1820 on. The centrepiece is Carlton Crescent, not quite a crescent but a curve with a slight pinch. The houses are austerely classical, in stucco, the most conspicuous being detached, but linked by screen walls, the whole making a fine series round the curve; one, in a key position, breaks out into a bow. Until lately its attribution was unknown; Mr Robert Coles has shown that the scheme was promoted by Edward Toomer and designed by his son Samuel. Toomer also probably designed the exquisite Carlton Lodge on the corner of Bedford Place, a classical composition full of fascinating detail – for instance the locally characteristic sunflower pattern in the arched recesses over the windows, and the big two-storeyed bow on the Bedford Place frontage. Carlton Crescent adjoins the site of the Ordnance Survey Office, where the finest detailed maps ever were produced from 1841 till 1940. Bombs then destroyed most of the buildings, but some survive incorporated into modern development. The Ordnance Survey is now in modern buildings on the outskirts of the city.

Finally, in the district of Highfield, east of the Common, is some of the country's finest suburban development of the inter-war years. It was designed by Herbert Collins who, as Mr Robert Williams describes in a recent book, came from London to Southampton after the first world war. Collins was influenced by Sir Raymond Unwin – the greatest housing architect of the day – at Letchworth and Hampstead Garden Suburb, and by Unwin's disciple Louis de Soissons at Welwyn Garden City. Collins' houses are usually in short terraces, of perhaps four or five, very much in an adaptation of the

24   **Carlton Crescent, Southampton**, part of the fashionable development of the 1820s, by Samuel Toomer.

Georgian vernacular style – that of cottages rather than grander town houses. He related his houses with the greatest care to each other and to the subtleties of their setting – to slopes in the ground, alignments of roads, and trees; Collins never removed a good tree unless it were unavoidable. Green spaces, grassed or tree-grown, make focal points. His principles are displayed almost to perfection in his houses of 1922–38 in Orchards Way, Uplands Way, Highfield Close and the adjoining part of Brookvale Road. He designed elsewhere in Southampton suburbs, for instance in Bassett Green (Ethelburt Avenue) and Swaything (along Mansbridge Road) but not with quite the same flair as in Orchards Way. If only more of the huge amount of inter-war and post-war housing had approached Collins' standards in design!

Stockbridge
Hampshire

Stockbridge has a single street, very wide, crossing the flat valley of the River Test on the route from Winchester to Salisbury. The river proper is at its western end, but several branch streams flow through the town, and can be seen here and there passing under the street. The street must have been laid out deliberately, possibly in about 1200 when a market charter was granted – very much as happened at Alresford at the same time (page 13). It is a real town in atmosphere and appearance, though so small; cars now park on the edges of the street where weekly market stalls would originally have been set up. The townscape is punctuated by the big buff-brick classical Town Hall of 1810, by the

Grosvenor Hotel nearly opposite, of similar date, with its very large first-floor projection over open columns, and by the spire of the Victorian church. This replaced a small ancient church at the far east end of the town, of which the chancel, recently restored, survives – it is approached beside one of the town's many inns, the White Hart, whose upper storey is supported on thin iron columns. The views along the street each way are closed by the low green slopes of the valley sides. Like Whitchurch, Petersfield and Haslemere, and Newtown and Yarmouth on the Isle of Wight, Stockbridge was a rotten borough and sent two members to Parliament up to 1832.

Titchfield

Hampshire

Titchfield is a surprisingly preserved old town in the developed area between Southampton and Portsmouth, near the mouth of the little River Meon, which till the seventeenth century had a small estuary reaching to the town. There was a market in Norman times, and in 1232 an abbey was founded about three-quarters of a mile to the north. At the Dissolution it was in the hands of Thomas Wriothesley, later Earl of Southampton, one of Henry VIII's agents in the disposal of monastic possessions. He converted the abbey into a mansion for himself, with a great stone gatehouse over part of the site of the church, a splendid example in the English tradition with corner turrets. Nearby are two Tudor chimneystacks which are among the earliest examples of decorative brickwork in the area. Close by

25 *Right* **Titchfield Abbey.** The Gatehouse was built *c*.1540 by Thomas Wriothesley, later Earl of Southampton (**28**), over the site of the abbey, for the dissolution of which he was agent. The elaborate chimneys provide one of the earliest examples of brickwork in Hampshire.

26 *Below* **Titchfield,** a former market town, preserves its identity in a fast developing part of Hampshire.

27   **Titchfield Abbey**. Gargoyles on the Tudor gatehouse (25).

28   **St Peter's Church, Titchfield**. Monument to Thomas Wriothesley, first Earl of Southampton (25), his Countess and their son, with members of the family on the side panels.

is a monastic barn with a fine roof, recently restored, now used as a farm shop. There were four earls of Southampton of the Wriothesley dynasty – the third was patron of Shakespeare. The fourth had a London house in Bloomsbury, the development of which he started; it was his heiress who married into the Russell family, bringing Bloomsbury into the possession of the Dukes of Bedford. Titchfield passed to other hands, and the house was ruinous by the mid-eighteenth century. Much of the town is still Tudor or early seventeenth-century in its fabric, with timber-framed and early brick houses, and others with Georgian fronts often concealing older work. There is an attractive pattern of narrow streets converging on the central wide street where, until the nineteenth century there stood a small timber-framed market hall with open-sided ground storey. This was dismantled, partly re-erected elsewhere, and, in the 1960s, re-erected again in the Weald and Downland museum at Singleton, near Chichester. It probably dates from the sixteenth century and provides an early instance of brick-nogging (bricks filling the timber framework) of which there are other examples in the town. The base of the church tower was a Saxon porch which may date from as early as AD 700. Inside there is a great tomb commemorating members of the Wriothesley family. Titchfield became overshadowed by Fareham in the eighteenth century because of the latter's better situation; it now has the status of a village, defiant against the encroaching development. (See colour illus. opp. p. 32.)

Whitchurch
Hampshire

Whitchurch grew where several routes converged beside the River Test. It was a rotten borough, returning members to Parliament from 1586 to the Reform Act of 1832. The streets make a shape like an irregular fivefold star, but the buildings do not always take advantage of this potentially attractive form. However the White Hart, built at the end of the coaching era, takes the sharp corner between two streets very well, with a Doric porch at the apex, topped by an iron balcony, and a plaster hart with antlers on the skyline.

The nearby Georgian Town Hall of red brick with a cupola has an arched ground storey now occupied by a bank. A restored jettied timber-framed house is a landmark in Newbury Street. But the town's great feature is the Silk Mill, built around 1800 on a much older mill site, and first used for weaving silk about thirty years later. It was recently bought and restored by the Hampshire Buildings Preservation Trust and is now managed by a trust backed by the local council. Silk fabrics continue to be woven on traditional machinery, and the great water wheel remains. The mill lies astride the apex of an island between the main stream of the Test and a branch; the principal block is of brick with iron-framed windows and a cupola – decent classical architecture adapted to early industry. It is regularly open and very popular.

The church, on the western edge of the town, successor to a Saxon 'white church' which may have been so called because it was of stone, not timber, is Victorian outside, but has a medieval core; its treasure is a Saxon sculpture of Christ in a rounded recess, discovered during the church's restoration in 1866 and said to date from the ninth century; a Latin inscription says that it commemorates a lady called Frithburga.

Wickham

Hampshire

Wickham has a splendid 'Square', probably laid out about 1268, when Roger de Scures, the lord of the manor, obtained a charter for a market and fair. (The town's most famous native, William of Wykeham, was born, apparently of humble parents, in 1324.) The size of the space was probably related to the annual fair, still held as a pleasure event in May, rather than the former market. By chance, the buildings around the Square compose a supremely effective picture. At the far end to the east are two Georgian houses, the nearer earlier and smaller, the further one plainer but providing a climax (**30**); both have striking doorcases. On the opposite side is a different build-up; first a pair of Georgian houses catches the eye (early semi-detached), then, near the corner, comes a house built like others in grey and red brick, but with a big canted bay on the first floor standing on pillars to provide a porch (**29**). Many of the other houses are older – timber-framed, but variously altered and re-fronted. At the far end the Square is divided by an island block. Bridge Street

29 The Square, Wickham. One of the many Georgian houses, in grey and red brick, which give distinction to the old towns of south-eastern Hampshire – unusual for its bay window over the porch.

30 *Left* **The Square, Wickham.** A very large space, probably laid out *c.*1268 when a charter for a market and fair was obtained. Though Georgian fronts are prominent, many of the houses are visibly older and timber-framed.

31 *Below* **Bridge Street, Wickham.** In the centre is Queen Lodge, originally 17th century, with details in carved brickwork, and later windows. In the background an altered timber-framed 'Wealden' house.

30 *Left* **The Square, Wickham.** A very large space, probably laid out *c.*1268 when a charter for a market and fair was obtained. Though Georgian fronts are prominent, many of the houses are visibly older and timber-framed.

descends to the east past a surprising variety of moderately-scaled domestic buildings. First there is a gabled flint-fronted Victorian house. Then, on the left, Queen Lodge, originally of the mid-seventeenth century, displaying a classical entablature and Ionic capitals in carved brick in the centre of the façade. It was altered in Georgian times, when sash windows replaced the original long window ranges, of which traces are evident (**31**). Then, past Georgian fronts, a partly timbered house closes the view; this was a fifteenth-century 'Wealden' house where the recessed centre, characteristic of that type of house, was later filled with a brick wall. Finally, astride the little River Meon, is Chesapeake Mill built in 1820; the outer walls are of brick but the internal timbers are partly from the United States ship *Chesapeake*, captured in the war of 1813 and broken up after serving for a few years with the Royal Navy.

Winchester

Hampshire

Winchester is one of the great medieval cities of Europe. Few others retain medieval buildings to compare, collectively, with the cathedral, castle hall, college and hospital of St Cross. Complementing these are hundreds of domestic and other buildings, medieval, Georgian and Victorian, along miles of historic streets, against the background of green hills.

There was a Roman town, *Venta Belgarum*, alongside a prehistoric site; of this the alignment of the High Street and the line of the city walls remain. It shrank to insignificance for a time after the Romans left. The first church was built *c*.645 becoming a cathedral in 676, when the kings of emergent Wessex probably had a palace there. King Alfred refortified the city in his struggle against the Vikings. Under him and his successors Winchester became the chief centre of the kingdom of Wessex which in time, through its north-ward and eastward expansion, became effectively that of England. The city was replanned within the strengthened Roman defences, with new streets leading off at fairly regular intervals north and south of High Street – they do not correspond with the lost Roman pattern of secondary streets, as archaeologists have proved. Under St Ethelwold, bishop from 963 to 984, the cathedral church was reformed as a Benedictine monastery which, like that at Canterbury, became famous for book and manuscript illustration. Adjoining the cathedral to the north was another monastery, the New Minster, and beyond that was St Mary's abbey for nuns. Together they must have formed the most impressive group of buildings in later Saxon England, except perhaps at Canterbury and possibly York. The Saxon cathedral stood north-west of the present cathedral, which was started in 1079, using stone from the Binstead quarries on the Isle of Wight (page 52). The bishopric was the richest in England, and its holders were often politically powerful. Bishop Henry of Blois built the now ruinous Wolvesey Castle as his fortified residence, and founded the Hospital of St Cross. He was deeply involved in the struggle between his brother King Stephen and the Empress Matilda, when much of Winchester was burnt, including the royal palace which stood south

32 *Right* **Winchester Cathedral**. The Saxon cathedral was on the grassy area, left foreground. The present cathedral was started 1079 with stone from the Isle of Wight. The west front was remodelled in the 14th century and the nave soon after by William of Wykeham. The interior is very much grander than the austere exterior suggests.

of High Street, close to the cathedral. But by then the castle had been built on higher ground to the west, partly as a royal residence; here Domesday Book was compiled, and the royal treasury kept till the end of the twelfth century. Henry III built the present Great Hall which is all that survives of the castle – internally the finest medieval hall in England except Westminster Hall. Comparison with Westminster is appropriate, since after the thirteenth century Winchester was no longer a royal residence and Westminster became, indisputably, the centre of the realm. Previously, for about two centuries, the functions and status of effective capital had been shared between Winchester and Westminster.

William of Wykeham, bishop from 1367 and for many years Chancellor of England, remodelled the cathedral nave, to the design of William Wynford – one of the great medieval architects (Henry Yevele is another) whose names are now known through documentary evidence, but who are not yet popularly recognized as architects of the calibre of Wren, as they ought to be. Wykeham founded Winchester College, which was at first intended primarily for boys who would pass on to his other foundation, New College, Oxford. But it set the pattern for numerous late medieval, Tudor and subsequent schools, not only large 'public' schools, but also smaller grammar schools in towns all round the country. The main buildings round the two courtyards, with the chapel and cloister, all designed by William Wynford, remain relatively little altered – with many others added in more recent times. Cardinal Beaufort, bishop from 1404, augmented Henry of Blois' Hospital of St Cross, and built the present pensioners' rooms and great hall in collegiate form, adjoining the earlier magnificent church – architecturally one of the most impressive medieval charitable foundations in England.

Much of the medieval glory of Winchester departed at the Reformation. Hyde Abbey, on the northern outskirts, which replaced the Saxon New Minster next to the cathedral in the twelfth century, was destroyed, as was St Mary's nunnery. Luckily the cathedral was retained, with dean and canons to replace the medieval monks: parts of the monastic buildings were converted into clerics' houses. The Civil War caused destruction too, both to the cathedral area and to the castle which, after being besieged, was finally 'slighted' (made useless militarily), and eventually cleared except for the Great Hall.

Winchester was already in economic decline before the Reformation. In its twelfth-century heyday its population may have been as much as 8,000 – making it among the largest towns in England. It was an early centre of weaving – the clothiers and weavers mainly operating in the north-eastern part of the city, called the Brooks, where there were many carefully channelled streams used for processing; the River Itchen provided power for fulling mills. Archaeological excavation in this area revealed, *inter alia*, remains of medieval merchants' premises and humbler weavers' homes. The whole of this part of the city became depopulated in the later Middle Ages because of the decline in the weaving trade. Nobody knows fully why the Winchester woollen industry, once so important, should have decayed so early, while that of Salisbury and numerous other places in the West of England, in East Anglia, and elsewhere was expanding so fast. But it did –

33 *Opposite* **Winchester College,** founded 1382 by Bishop Wykeham and designed by William Wynford, provided a prototype for many, often much smaller, grammar and public schools.

and this, combined with the loss of Winchester's status as royal capital, the destruction of the abbeys, and the eclipse of the once very important annual St Giles's Fair, led to a reduction in population to about 2,000–3,000 in the early seventeenth century.

Winchester had both a Restoration and a Renaissance in the late seventeenth century. The cathedral close was reconstructed after the restoration of the monarchy and the re-establishment of the Anglican hierarchy. Charles II decided to build a new palace on part of the castle site, an English version of Versailles, with Wren as architect. It was largely completed, but not fitted, when he died; it was later converted to barracks and finally destroyed by fire. But the building of the palace had a stimulating effect on Winchester which was lasting. Charles stayed there, with his courtiers, on several occasions when the palace was building, and the city became established as a fashionable place to live. Bishop Morley started a new palace adjacent to ruinous Wolvesey Castle – but, like his immediate predecessors, his successors preferred to live in Farnham Castle rather than Winchester itself, and it was not till modern times that Wolvesey Palace again became the permanent home of the bishops. Many other well-to-do people settled in the city, and one of the delights of Winchester is the large number of late Stuart and early Georgian houses, usually of the deep red local brick, sometimes interspersed with grey. Perhaps the city languished a little as a favoured place of residence in later Georgian times, when Southampton became more fashionable, but it had another spurt in early Victorian times – the railway, on the way to Southampton, arrived early; there were trains from London by 1840. But Victorian Winchester

34 *Above left* **Winchester Cathedral** seen from the ruins of the Norman and later Wolvesey Castle, the medieval residence of the bishops.

35 *Above right* **High Street, Winchester** follows the Roman line, with some distortion in the early medieval period, and has buildings of every subsequent date; the one with a big round-headed window was a Georgian inn, the bank is a conversion of the Guildhall of 1713 – with a statue of Queen Anne and a projecting clock. In the far distance is the medieval Westgate (*see colour illus. opp. p. 33*).

36 *Opposite* **Hospital of St Cross, Winchester.** The back of the brethren's apartments of *c.*1445.

never grew substantially. Today, county administration looms large, physically and socially, but Winchester has become once again a desirable place to live in. It is very much on the defensive against being swamped by the development of the burgeoning Southampton–Solent area, and by the traffic heading there. It is visibly conservation-conscious, and walks through its extensive better parts can be an almost continuous delight. Any description of Winchester in a short space must be extremely cursory, and is covered under the following headings: *High Street – Westgate to Eastgate; the Cathedral Close; South of High Street; East of the River; North of High Street.*

High Street – Westgate to Eastgate

The Westgate is best seen from further down High Street, where it still appears to close the street. The effect has been ruined near at hand since the traffic sweeps round one side, leaving the gate to appear to project from the buildings on the other side, a setting that is somehow less satisfactory than that of the Bargate at Southampton, stranded though that is in a complete roundabout. The Westgate is less grand than the Bargate though evidently remodelled at about the same time; the late fourteenth-century outer front is in the same style as that of the Bargate. All around are county buildings, illustrating how the county government developed out of the royal courts at the castle. From the fourteenth century, local justices of the peace sat at Quarter Sessions which were usually held, four times annually, in the Great Hall of the castle – like the Assizes, to which the High Court judges came twice yearly. Serious criminal cases were tried at the Assizes, less serious ones at Quarter Sessions, which also dealt with county business. When elected county councils were set up in 1888, they took on the administrative functions of Quarter Sessions, as well as others. The scope of county government steadily expanded until it reached a peak in the 1960s, and this is reflected at Winchester. Fairly modest buildings in vernacular Tudor or Jacobean styles were built between the restored Great Hall and Westgate in the late nineteenth and early twentieth centuries. In 1959–60 a large new block, based on an inter-war design, was built east of the Westgate – in deep red brick, and in a style which seemed hopelessly traditionalist to the modernists when it was opened, but which is more acceptable today. Later additions in modern styles are less so.

Below the Westgate, High Street steadily takes shape, especially past the staggered crossroads, beset with traffic, where Southgate Street leads off to the right and Jewry Street to the left. The delightful sinuous Georgian shop front of the equally old *Hampshire Chronicle* is a portent of the dense variety of frontages – though often only over shop level – along the rest of High Street, which is mostly now pedestrianized. A great deal is Georgian, with some pleasant bow windows; some is Victorian, like the elaborate building, originally a pub, at the corner of St Thomas Street, by the local architect Thomas Stopher; some is make-believe Tudor, like the façade of the otherwise genuinely Tudor God Begot House. Lloyds Bank is a remodelling of the modest former Guildhall of 1713, with a projecting clock, resembling that at Guildford. Mention of Guildford is appropriate, for in the distance beyond the end of the street, as at Guildford, a green hill rises – here it is St Giles Hill, where the ancient fair was held. The central landmark of High Street is

the fifteenth-century Butter Cross, where the street widens (see col. illus. opp. p. 33). It is one of few of its kind surviving – a huge Gothic pinnacle embellished with a host of lesser pinnacles and niches, elevated above steps round which butter sellers are said to have stood, hence the name. It is much restored but lucky to survive at all. The larger and different Cross at Chichester is a slightly later development of the theme. Behind the Butter Cross is a plausibly late medieval house, gabled and jettied, and next is another, probably once like it but plastered and Georgianized – not necessarily less interesting on that account. Nearby is a passageway through to the cathedral area. High Street then narrows; on the right is the Pentice, first the site of the royal palace, then of a mint, then of a drapery market, but by the fifteenth century occupied by merchants' houses. Some are as early, though much altered; two retain original bargeboards on their gables. They all project over the pavement, supported on pillars with modern shops set behind – like the Butterwalks at Totnes and Dartmouth. Here High Street is very busy; property values rise; it then broadens with the Victorian Gothic Guildhall (1871–3) on the right. The widest part – called Broadway – is dominated by the supremely effective statue of King Alfred, arm outstretched, by Hamo Thornycroft (1901). Beyond this the Eastgate stood, demolished like two other town gates for Georgian road improvements. But a later road improvement – the construction of Eastgate Street in the 1840s – resulted in real gain, since the bow-fronted houses on the rounded corner with Broadway, in latter-day Regency style, provide a marvellous interplay of curves.

The Cathedral Close

The Close is south of the cathedral – it developed after the Reformation out of the old monastic precinct – and is approached intricately from the west or the east. The eastern approach is more revealing – beginning in Colebrook Street behind the Guildhall, which has some fine Georgian houses. A path passes a formal watery garden outside the Lady Chapel at the furthest end of the cathedral, and then bends between walls of stone, flint and brick to

38 *Above* **10 The Close, Winchester,** altered after the Reformation from a monastic building into a cathedral cleric's house.

39 *Right* **Kingsgate Street, Winchester,** a slightly sinuous street with Georgian fronts (some of the houses are older behind).

emerge where the cloister was, now an open grassy space extending irregularly southward, surrounded loosely by cathedral clergy houses, which were either rebuilt or considerably restored in the late seventeenth and early eighteenth centuries, following the depredations of the Civil War and Commonwealth; their history is described in John Crook's *The Wainscot Book*. Some retain medieval parts. The Anglican cathedral close is something not paralleled outside England and Wales: no other country had an established church with an essentially Catholic hierarchy of bishops, deans, canons and other clergy, and allowed them to marry; hence its unique clerical-domestic character; Winchester has one of the most delightful examples. Three vignettes summarize the quality of the Close. First, the view of the Deanery (see col. illus. opp. p. 33) with its exquisite three-arched porch, built for the prior's house which preceded it; its fourteenth-century hall since subdivided, with a plain Georgian end wall; and a long low brick wing behind – built at about the time when Charles II stayed with the Dean while his palace was being built. Second, the cul-de-sac called Dome Alley: four pairs of houses built for canons in the 1660s, with carved brickwork on their gables; the view is closed by the fine Victorian spire of St Thomas' church. Third, at the southern end of the Close, Cheyney Court, with three picturesque timber-framed gables rising above a flinty ground storey. The gables, like the restored windows, look Jacobean, dating from the end of the timber-framing tradition. Nearby is the southern gate out of the Close.

South of High Street

There is a network of little streets south of the middle part of High Street –

40 *Right* **Chesil Street, Winchester,** showing apparently Georgian houses, and one of the city's formerly numerous small churches, St Peter Chesil (for the backs of these houses see **42**).

41 *Below* **St Cross Hospital, Winchester,** founded in 1136; the hall and gatehouse date from *c.*1445.

part of the Saxon grid – with a thick scatter of pleasant, well-tended Georgian houses, and of recent infillings and conversions, reflecting the welcome trend for people to move back to the inner city, from which there has been so much recent depopulation. St Thomas Street is the most typical of these streets, but Southgate Street, wider and busier, has the two best houses. One, the present Southgate Hotel of 1715, has columns and other motifs in carved brickwork. The other, Serles House, set back and now a military museum, is

of about the same date but more sophisticated, with a great curved projecting centrepiece, also with brick pilasters, eminently baroque and attributed to the architect Thomas Archer. St Swithun's Street leads down past more Georgian houses and the medieval Close wall to the south gate of the Close, already described. This stands, intriguingly, at right angles to one of the two remaining city gates, Kingsgate, with a miniature church above. Outside is the area dominated by the College; the long and delightful Kingsgate Street runs with a slightly sinuous line and assorted Georgian façades (with some older evidence) towards the unique medieval Hospital of St Cross (**36 41**). It is remarkable that both the College and the more distant St Cross should be outside the city wall. College Street leads, from Kingsgate itself, past the entrance to the College and then that to Wolvesey Palace (with the ruined Wolvesey Castle behind) into a delightful area. A path curves past the one remaining length of the city wall, a plain patchwork of flint and occasional rubble stone. On the right is the river.

East of the river
There was always – at least since Norman times – a populous suburb across the River Itchen. It is best seen first across the river, from the path described above. The narrow and strangely unpolluted river is backed by a series of garden walls in a medley of stonework, flint and brick. Behind are long gardens extending to the picturesque backs of houses which face Chesil Street – described shortly – and are on the whole older than they appear from that street. To the right is the picturesque tower of St Peter Chesil church, unusually tile-hung. Such domestic gardens behind street frontages were once very characteristic of old towns; too often now they have become commercial yards or car parks, or have disappeared under development. To reach the front of the houses one crosses the small stone bridge at the end of High Street and its continuation Broadway, with the converted brick and tiled City Mill of 1744 to the north. Chesil Street (**40**) is traffic-ridden, but it makes a fine picture with the Georgian-fronted houses on the right – whose gardens run down to the river (**42**) – the two-gabled fifteenth-century Old Chesil restaurant on the left and the little church closing the view. Winchester once had many small churches like this but few survive – many disappeared even before the end of the Middle Ages. The best remaining parish church in the city is nearby St John's – reached along narrow St John's Street, recently revived after decay. This has a striking thirteenth-century geometrical window, and from the churchyard there is a good view back over the city.

North of High Street
There is less to see north of High Street, but some of the parallel side streets, of Saxon origin, are interesting. St Peter's Street has fine late seventeenth- and early eighteenth-century houses in brick. Jewry Street with its double twist is full of variety; it is predominantly nineteenth-century, including two parts of what was the prison, of 1804, and grim incised quoin stones on what are now the upper storeys of shops, with a Victorian Congregational church in between. The dominant feature is the old Corn Exchange, now the public

42 Back of Chesil Street, Winchester, showing the houses in (**40**) and the tile-hung tower of the church; many of the houses are older than their fronts suggest. Large gardens, unsuspected from the streets, were characteristic of old towns. In the foreground the River Itchen, and a wall with patchwork materials.

library, an inventive classical building of 1838 with a portico recalling Inigo Jones' church in Covent Garden, and recently cleaned walls of creamy brick. It is by Owen Carter, an outstanding local architect, who designed classical terraces and Gothic churches. In contrast is a building further north on the opposite side, fluent with little gables and iron balconies, by Stopher, Carter's successor as the leading local architect. Also striking is the latest building in the street, Sheridan House, by the locally-based architect Robert Adam, in a style inspired by Victorian warehouses, with great brick arches containing shop fronts and first-floor windows – something for which there is no particular precedent in Winchester, but which fits in perfectly.

Yarmouth
Isle of Wight

Although a place called Ermud, identified as Yarmouth, was mentioned in the Domesday Book, it seems that Yarmouth, as a town, was founded about 1170 by Richard de Redvers, the lord of the island, just before Newport (page 34). It was sacked by the French in 1377 and several times later, and never fully recovered, although unlike neighbouring Newtown it remained a small port, and is now the terminal for the ferry from Lymington. It has a grid plan with central wide street or 'Square', running south to the church – a simple Gothic building of about 1625, with a tall tower top of 1831, added as a landmark from the sea. The town's buildings show a nice variety of materials. Many are faced in rough Island stone, brownish in colour; others are in the dark red local brick, such as the plain Town Hall protruding from one side of the Square. The long narrow High Street, leading east, is the most attractive in the town; it begins with a few shops, but for most of its length it has a succession of fairly simple, mainly Georgian houses faced in stone, brick or stucco, not always continuous but often separated by garden walls along the street, shaded by trees. A few alleys lead north to end on the foreshore. In the other direction, Quay Street runs past what is now the George hotel, built by Sir Robert Holmes, Governor of the Isle, who died in 1692 – he is buried in a side chapel of the church. The hotel abuts on to Yarmouth Castle which on the other side faces the sea – finished in 1547 as one of the last of Henry VIII's forts. Inside is seventeenth-century brickwork, related to the former domestic quarters of the garrison. On the southern fringe of the town is the former tide mill – three-storeyed, of brick, and perhaps the best preserved of what was once a fairly common type of building round the creeks of the Solent. It borders a marsh-bound creek.

Bibliography

General
A History of Hampshire, B. Carpenter Turner, 1978
A History of Surrey, P. Brandon, 1977
The Isle of Wight. An Illustrated History, J. and J. Jones, 1987
Hampshire and the Isle of Wight, N. Pevsner and D.W. Lloyd, 1967; Buildings of England series
Surrey, I. Nairn and N. Pevsner, revised B. Cherry, 1971; Buildings of England series
Hampshire, The Complete Guide, J. Draper, 1990
Wight, Portrait of an Island, P. Hyland, 1984
The Portsmouth Region, ed. B. Stapleton and J.H. Thomas, 1989
Historic Architecture of the Royal Navy, J.G. Coad, 1983
The English Medieval Town, C. Platt, 1976; material on Winchester and Southampton
New Towns of the Middle Ages, M.W. Beresford, 1967; ref. Alresford, Haslemere, Lymington, Newport, Newtown, Petersfield, Portsmouth, Reigate, Stockbridge, Yarmouth
Medieval England, M.W. Beresford and J.K. St. Joseph, 1979; air photographs, etc. of Newtown and Yarmouth, Isle of Wight
Medieval Hall Houses of the Winchester Area, E. Lewis, E. Roberts and K. Roberts, 1988
The Surrey Style, R. Gradidge, 1991; revival of vernacular styles
Old West Surrey, G. Jekyll, 1904; reprinted
Old Towns Revisited, ed. A. Oswald, 1952; article on Farnham by C. Hussey
Farmhouses and Cottages in the Isle of Wight, M. Brinton, 1987; material relevant to towns

Books on individual towns
Andover, A Historical Portrait, J. Spaul, 1977
Croydon, A Pictorial History, J.B. Gent, 1991
History of Emsworth and Warblington, A.J.C. Reger, 1967
The Story of Gosport, L. White, revised 1989
Guildford, E.R. Chamberlin, 1982
Kingston's Past Rediscovered, J. Wakeford, 1990
Portsmouth, a history, A. Temple Patterson, 1976
The Spirit of Portsmouth, ed. J. Webb, S. Quail, P. Haskell and R. Riley, 1989
Buildings of Portsmouth and its Environs, D.W. Lloyd, 1974
Medieval Southampton, C. Platt, 1973
Bygone Southampton, J. Stovold, 1984
Southampton, An Illustrated History, A. Rance, 1986

Titchfield, A Place in History, ed. R. Wade and G. Watts, 1989
Winchester, B. Carpenter Turner, 1980
The Ancient Town of Yarmouth, C.W.R. Winter, 1981

Booklets on individual towns
Explore Christchurch, K. and S. Jarvis
A Thousand Years of Christchurch, R.A. Lavender
Central Croydon, B.J. Salter
Old Emsworth; The Emsworth Oyster Fleet and other titles by D.J. Rudkin
Epsom Town, Downs and Common, B.J. Salter
The Story of Godalming, J. Janaway
Godalming 400, D. Coombs
The Story of Lymington, R. Coles
Odiham High Street, an Itinerary, Odiham Society
Petersfield in Tudor Times and other titles by Petersfield Area Historical Society
Old Romsey at Work and other titles by Lower Test Valley Archaeological Trust
The Story of Romsey, P. Berrow, B. Burbridge, P. Genge
Wayfarers' Winchester, R. Hubbuck

Paperbacks in large format
Hampshire's Heritage; Hampshire County Council
The Archaeology of Hampshire, ed. S.J. Shennan and R.T. Schalda Hall, 1981
The Small Towns of Hampshire. The Archaeological and Historical Implications of Development, M. Hughes, 1976
Historic Towns in Surrey, M. O'Connell, 1977
Lymington, B.J. Down, 1989
High Street, Petersfield, 1984; detailed study by Petersfield Area Historical Society
A Military Heritage. A History of Portsmouth Town Fortifications, B.H. Patterson, 1984
Fort Nelson and the Portsmouth Forts, G. Mitchell and F. Cobb, 1987
A.E. Cogswell, architect within a Victorian city; reprint of dissertation by A. Nash, 1975; Portsmouth Polytechnic School of Architecture
Southampton's Historic Buildings, R.J. Coles, 1981
A Prospect of Winchester, A. Rance, 1978
Winchester Castle and Great Hall, M. Biddle and B. Clayre, 1983

The *Portsmouth Papers* are published by Portsmouth City Council. The following are specially relevant (titles sometimes shortened):
1. *Portchester Castle*, B. Cunliffe, 1967/84

3. *Palmerston's Folly*, A. Temple Patterson, 1967/85; Victorian forts
8. *Portsea Island Churches*, R. Hubbuck, revised 1976
16. *The Growth of Southsea*, R.C. Riley, 1972
30. *The Western Defences of Portsmouth Harbour*, G.H. Williams, 1979; relates to Gosport
32. *The Houses and Inhabitants of Thomas Ellis Owen's Southsea*, R.C. Riley, 1980
38. *Public Houses and Beerhouses in Nineteenth Century Portsmouth*, R.C. Riley, 1983
44. *The Evolution of the Docks and Buildings in Portsmouth Royal Dockyard*, R.C. Riley, 1985
48. *The Industrial Archaeology of the Portsmouth Region*, R.C. Riley, 1987
58. *The Demise of Demon Drink? Portsmouth Pubs 1900–50*, P. Eley and R.C. Riley, 1991

Town trails and walks

The following are recommended: *Andover Town Trail, Fareham Town Walks, Historic Farnham, A Godalming Walk, Explore Guildford, Havant Town Trail, Kingston Town Centre Walk, Reigate Town Trail, Romsey Town Trail, Titchfield Village Walk, Wickham; A Perambulation*

Index

The black and white photographs are shown in the Index in **bold** under plate numbers